A CHORUS OF DISAPPROVAL

First produced at the Stephen Joseph Theatre in the Round, Scarborough, on 22nd May, 1984, with the following cast:

Guy Jones	Lennox Greaves
Dafydd ap Llewellyn	Russell Dixon
Hannah Llewellyn	Alwyne Taylor
Bridget Baines	Jane Hollowood
Mr Ames	Paul Todd
Enid Washbrook	Dorcas Jones
Rebecca Huntley-Pike	Heather Stoney
Fay Hubbard	Lesley Meade
Ian Hubbard	Mark Jax
Jarvis Huntley-Pike	Alan Thompson
Ted Washbrook	Robert Cotton
Crispin Usher	Daniel Flynn
Linda Washbrook	Caroline Webster
Raymond	
Stage Managers (non-speaking)	

The play directed by Alan Ayckbourn
Setting by Edward Lipscomb
Musical Direction by Paul Todd

The action occurs between the first rehearsal and first performance of an amateur production of Gay's *The Beggar's Opera* (Feb-May). It takes place in and around a small provincial theatre

Subsequently presented in the Olivier auditorium of the National Theatre on 1st August, 1985, with the following cast:

Guy Jones	Bob Peck
Dafydd ap Llewellyn	Michael Gambon
Hannah Llewellyn	Imelda Staunton
Bridget Baines	Jenny Galloway
Mr Ames	Paul Todd
Enid Washbrook	Jane Wenham
Rebecca Huntley-Pike	Moira Redmond
Fay Hubbard	Gemma Craven
Ian Hubbard	Paul Bentall
Jarvis Huntley-Pike	David Ryall
Ted Washbrook	James Hayes
Crispin Usher	Daniel Flynn
Linda Washbrook	Kelly Hunter

Directed by Alan Ayckbourn
Settings by Alan Tagg
Music Director Paul Todd

MUSIC FOR "THE BEGGAR'S OPERA"

The score used for the musical numbers from *The Beggar's Opera* in the original productions of *A Chorus of Disapproval* was the Frederick Austin version published by Boosey and Hawkes (1920 revised 1926) and companies performing the play are advised to obtain this.

ACT I

The Lights come up abruptly on a stage filled with people and we are suddenly and unexpectedly into the final moments of a first performance of an amateur production of Gay's "The Beggar's Opera". The performance by P.A.L.O.S. (The Pendon Amateur Light Operatic Society) is filled with gusto and enthusiasm. What it lacks in polish (in some quarters) it makes up for in flourish. Among the performers is, centre on a small raised platform, Guy Jones (Macheath). He is surrounded by his "doxies". Amongst these are Hannah Llewellyn (Polly Peachum), Linda Washbrook (Lucy Lockit), Rebecca Huntley-Pike (Mrs Vixen), Fay Hubbard (Dolly Trull), Bridget Baines (Jenny Diver) and others. Also present are Ted and Enid Washbrook (Mr and Mrs Peachum), Ian Hubbard (Matt of the Mint), Crispin Usher (Filch), Jarvis Huntley-Pike (Lockit) and others. At the piano, Mr Ames (The Beggar)

Guy (*as Macheath; singing*)
    Thus I stand like the Turk, with his doxies around;
    From all sides their glances his passion confound;
    For black, brown and fair, his inconstancy burns,
    And the different beauties subdue him by turns:
    Each calls forth her charms to provoke his desires:
    Though willing to all; with but one he retires.
    But think of this maxim, and put off your sorrow,
    The wretch of to-day, may be happy to-morrow.

All (*singing*)   Each calls forth her charms and provokes his desires,
    Though willing to all; with but one he retires.
    But think of this maxim, and put off your sorrow,
    The Wretch of to-day, may be happy tomorrow.

The dance that accompanies the final chorus finally finishes with a triumphant tableau. The Lights darken slightly to indicate the curtain has fallen. The company shuffle quickly into fresh positions. Muffled applause is heard. The Lights brighten as the curtain goes up and the applause becomes louder and clearer. The company are all smiles at once. Several of these pre-rehearsed variants follow with finally Guy as Macheath taking a solo call and being applauded by his fellow artistes. Graciously, he presents his two leading ladies, Hannah (Polly) and Linda (Lucy). Both, in turn, are presented with bouquets. Next, the company turn in the direction of Mr Ames (The Beggar)

*at the piano who rises and makes a sheepish acknowledgement. The general
bow follows*

> *At this point, with a sort of reluctant alacrity, the producer, Dafydd
> Llewellyn, springs on to the stage from the auditorium*

*The cast, in turn, applaud him. Looking somewhat incongruous in his modern
clothes, he bows modestly and finally raises his hands for silence. The applause
ceases*

Dafydd Ladies and gentleman, thank you all for that wonderful, wonderful
reception. There are a million people I ought to thank. There are a million
people I'd like to thank and there are a million people I'm afraid I'm not
going to thank, at least by name or you'll be sitting here till tomorrow
morning. (*He laughs*)

The cast smile with relief

> I will, if I may, restrict myself to saying this. Thank you, wonderful cast.
> Thank you, wonderful, wonderful stage management. Thank you, mar-
> vellous audience. But thank you most of all to one individual without
> whom none of this could have happened. He joined PALOS but a few
> weeks ago. The emergency occurred and the man rose to the occasion.
> What more can I say?—he's been ... Well, your reception said it all.
> Ladies and gentlemen, our very special Macheath, Mr Guy Jones.

*Dafydd turns and presents Guy who acknowledges fresh applause. Again, the
cast join in. The curtain falls finally. The Lights again dim to indicate this and
the applause becomes muffled, finally dying out*

> *The cast start to disperse, chattering and laughing and moving towards the
> dressing rooms*

*Guy, quite suddenly, is all alone. No one, once the curtain has fallen, speaks or
even acknowledges him. He stands for a moment before starting to remove his
costume, beginning with his wig and hat, then jacket and cravat*

> *Stage managers begin to move round him re-setting and striking props,
> including the raised platform*

*In time, the remaining stage lights go out and are replaced by harsh working
lights. Similarly the stage reverts from a performance to a rehearsal state*

> *Hannah, still in her basic Polly costume, comes on carrying Guy's ordinary
> clothes. She watches him for a second*

Hannah (*softly*) Well done.
Guy Mmm?
Hannah Well done.
Guy (*dully*) Thank you.
Hannah (*indicating his clothes*) Here are your ...

Guy makes no move

> I'll leave them here ... (*She puts the clothes gently on a table and makes to
> leave*)

Guy Thanks.

Hannah (*turning as she goes*) I—(*changing her mind*) Right. I must ...
Goodbye.

Guy Yes. Goodbye.

Hannah goes

*Guy finishes changing, finally putting on his mac. He seems about to leave but
turns in the doorway and surveys the darkened stage. We hear the distant
sound of the piano playing "Youth's the Season Made for Joys". It's a fragment,
a wistful echo of his memory*

*It is now three to four months earlier. February and very cold. Voices and
laughter are heard from a distance in the dressing rooms offstage. Guy, having
entered from the street, stands uncertainly wondering whether to proceed
further*

> *Bridget, in coat, hat and boots, enters with a small rehearsal table which she
> bangs down rather noisily*

*At first appearance she is a rather graceless, galumphing girl who has long ago
dispensed with social niceties and conventional sexual role-playing. She gives
no sign of having seen Guy but continues on her way. Guy makes a little
gurgling sound in his throat*

Bridget (*turning back at the last minute*) Did you want somebody?

Guy Mr Jones.

Bridget Mr Jones?

Guy Yes.

Bridget No.

Guy No?

Bridget No. No Mr Jones here.

Guy No, no ...

Bridget This is the Operatic Society.

Guy Yes, yes.

Bridget We haven't any Mr Jones.

Guy No. You won't have.

Bridget No?

Guy Well, you might have but ... No, I'm Mr Jones.

Bridget You're Mr Jones?

Guy Yes. (*Slight pause*) Sorry.

Bridget We'll start again, shall we?

Guy Yes.

Bridget I've just come in. Right?

Guy Right.

Bridget OK. So. Who do you want?

Guy Mr Lewellyn. Mr—(*he takes an envelope from his pocket and looks at
it*)—Mr D ap Llewellyn.

Bridget Is he expecting you?

Guy Yes, I think so. He said round about this time.

Bridget Wait there, then. Mr Jones, yes?

Guy Yes.

Bridget goes

Guy hops around a little. Half because of nerves, half because of the cold. He spies a piano in the corner and moves to it. From the envelope he is holding he produces a small piece of music, obviously torn from a book. With an inexperienced finger, he taps out the odd note and attempts to match them with his voice. Whatever he plays appears to be outside his range. He clears his throat but it's quite obvious that his voice has packed up completely. With sudden determination, Guy screws up the piece of music, stuffs it into his pocket and marches towards the door

Before he can leave, there is a burst of chatter from off and Dafydd enters. He is a busy, slightly overweight, energetic man in his late thirties. A live wire. The mainspring of the Society. Never using one word where three will do, never walking when he can hurry. Whatever the temperature, Dafydd always appears to find it a little on the warm side

Dafydd (*seeing Guy*) My dear chap, I'm so sorry. I'm deeply sorry. I knew you were coming. I wrote down you were coming. It slipped my mind. How do you do? Dafydd ap Llewellyn. Good of you to come along. We're on our first stages of rehearsal. Just getting started. Broken for tea for ten minutes.

Guy Ah. Yes.

Dafydd (*calling*) Mr Ames? I'll just fetch Mr Ames in and he can play for you. Brought something along to sing, have you?

Guy Well, I had sort of—

Dafydd (*calling*) Mr Ames? Otherwise we've got plenty of bits and pieces lying around, you know. And, of course, Mr Ames, he's encyclopaedic. He's played practically every musical comedy you could name. Choose a key, choose a tune, choose a tempo, he's away—where, the bloody hell is he? Excuse me. (*He moves to the door, calling*) Mr Ames?—ah, there you are. This is Mr Ames.

Mr Ames enters. He is a small, intensely shy man whose silent, unobtrusive personality is in direct contrast to that of Dafydd's

Mr Ames, this is Mr—God, I'm afraid I don't even know your name— Mr . . .?

Guy Jones.

Dafydd Mr Jones. Not Welsh, are you?

Guy No. No. 'Fraid not. From Leeds.

Dafydd (*dubiously*) Leeds?

Guy Originally.

Dafydd Originally from Leeds. Right. This is our Mr Ames. Mr Ames, Mr Jones is going to sing for us. Give us an idea of his range. And intonation. Which is a polite way of saying can he sing in tune. (*He laughs*) If not, welcome to the club. What are you, tenor, are you?

Guy I think I'm a sort of light baritone. I think.

Dafydd Oh yes? Light baritone, eh? Yes, we've got plenty of those lurking in the back row, haven't we, Mr Ames? They're what we call our down the octave brigade.

Guy (*laughing*) Yes, yes . . .

Dafydd Come on then. Let's have a listen. Did you say you had some music? Or shall we ask Mr Ames to rifle through his golden treasure chest of memories?

Guy (*fumbling for his music*) No, I've brought . . . (*He is unable to find it and rummages through his pockets*) Just a second . . .

Dafydd Bit of *Merry Widow*? Fancy that?

Guy (*somewhat panic-stricken at the thought*) No, no, please . . .

Dafydd *West Side Story? Oklahoma? The King and I?*

Mr Ames plays a bar of this last

Guy (*finding his music at last*) No. Here we are. Found it. Here. (*He holds up the crumpled piece of music*)

Dafydd Is that it?

Guy Sorry.

Dafydd You shouldn't have splashed out like that, you know. Not just for an audition. (*He laughs again*)

Dafydd takes the scrap of music from Guy and gives it to Mr Ames

Here we are, Mr Ames. Second Act of *Tannhauser* by the look of it. (*He laughs*) No, I'm sorry, Mr Jones. We're only having a little joke. Don't mind us, you'll get used to it. Possibly. (*Briskly*) Right. Seriously for a moment. Be serious, Llewellyn, boy. What have we got here? (*He puts on his reading glasses*) My word, my word. You still claim you're not Welsh? What does that say there, Mr Ames? What does it say to you? *All Through the Night.* Ar hyd y nos.

Guy Yes. Coincidence.

Dafydd (*mock serious*) Well. I don't know. Should we allow a man from Leeds to sing this, Mr Ames? Eh? What do you think?

Guy It was just the only song I happen to . . .

Dafydd Well. Seeing your name is Jones. Maybe. Special dispensation, eh?

Guy (*gamely trying to keep up with the joke*) Thank you very much . . .

Dafydd Just this once.

Guy It was the only song I knew in the piano stool. My mother used to sing it. Years ago.

Dafydd Your mother's Welsh, then?

Guy No.

Dafydd But she sings?

Guy No, she . . .

Dafydd Bring her down. Bring her down next time with you.

Guy No, she's dead.

Dafydd (*sadly*) Ah. Well. Too late, then. Too late. Sad. Can you play that do you think, Mr Ames?

Mr Ames Yes, yes . . . (*He plays a chord or two, peering at the music*)

*Enid Washbrook appears in the doorway during this. Behind Enid, her
daughter Linda cranes round her to catch a glimpse of the newcomer*

Enid Are we starting again, Dafydd?
Dafydd In just one moment, Enid, just one moment. We'll give you a call.
We're just going to hear this gentleman sing . . .
Enid Oh, right. Excuse us, won't you . . .
Dafydd We'll give you a call.
Enid (*to Guy, as they go*) Good luck.
Guy Thank you.

Enid and Linda go out

Dafydd Now, Mr Jones, the millon dollar question. Are you going to sing
this in Welsh or in English?
Guy Well, I'm sorry, in English if that's all right . . .
Dafydd (*hopping about in mock pain*) Oh, oh, oh, oh . . . Like *Pomp and
Circumstance* in Japanese . . . If you must, if you must . . . Right. When
you're ready, Mr Ames. Take it away . . .

*Mr Ames plays the introduction. Dafydd moves away slightly. Guy opens his
mouth to sing. Before he can do so, Dafydd is there before him sounding off in
a full Welsh tenor*

(*Singing*)   Holl amrantau'r ser ddywedant, Ar hyd y nos,
                Dyma'r ffordd i fro gogon-iant, Ar hyd y nos;
                Go-lau a-rall yw tywyll-wch, I arddangos gwir bryd-
                     ferthwch,
                Teulu'r nefoedd mewn ta-welwch, Ar hyd y nos.

Dafydd stops singing. Mr Ames stops playing. There is a respectful silence

Sorry. I'm sorry. I sincerely beg your pardon, Mr Jones. Every time I hear
. . . (*He breaks off too moved to continue. Then, clapping Guy on the
shoulder*) It's all yours. Take it away, boy.
Guy (*horrified*) Right.

*Mr Ames re-starts the introduction. Dafydd moves away to the far reaches of
the auditorium. Guy, by now very nervous, misses the introduction first time
round but manages on the second*

(*Nervously*)   While the moon her watch is keeping,
                    All through the night,
                While the we—
Dafydd (*calling from the darkness*) Mr Jones, sorry to interrupt you just as
you were getting underway. That's lovely. Very pleasant. A little tip. Just
try facing out this way a bit more, would you? You're not in need of the
music, are you?
Guy (*straining to see Dafydd*) No, no.
Dafydd No, it didn't appear you were reading it. (*Waving Guy away from
the safety of the piano*) Now. Just try placing your weight equally on both
your feet. Legs slightly apart. That's it. A bit more. Now, can you feel
yourself balanced, can you?

Guy Yes, yes.

Dafydd Singing is a great deal to do with balance, Mr Jones. Balance, you see. You can't sing on one leg now, can you? You'd feel unbalanced.

Guy Yes, yes.

Dafydd Good. Shoulders back, then. Shoulders right back, man.

Guy Yes.

Dafydd That's better. That's better. Now, before you start thist time, Mr Jones. I want you for a moment to breathe, if you would. Like this. (*He demonstrates noisily from the darkness*) In through the nose, you see, out through the mouth. That's it. And again. Deep as you can, that's it.

Guy sways and staggers

No, no. There's no need to hyperventilate. Breathe normally, that's all. Now, Mr Jones, can you feel all that air, can you? In your passages? Can you feel it rushing along your passages?

Guy Yes, yes.

Dafydd Blowing the cobwebs from your passages?

Guy (*coughing slightly*) Yes.

From this point, people begin to assemble, unseen by Guy, to listen to him. First to appear are Jarvis Huntley-Pike and Ted Washbrook. Jarvis is a man in his late fifties—the epitome of a Knowing Northerner. Ted, ten years younger, is a mild, pleasant, abstracted, ineffectual man

Dafydd Now you look like a real singer, Mr Jones. From the top, please, Mr Ames. From the top

Mr Ames starts again

(*Over the introduction*) Let it flow out of you, Mr Jones. Let it flow. It's a song that sings itself, you see. Like a river. (*Singing*) Holl amrantau'r ... You see?

Guy Yes, yes. (*He waits for the introduction to come round again*)

Fay Hubbard and Enid Washbrook enter and stand watching. Fay is an extremely attractive woman in her thirties. One of the local younger married jet-set. Enid, a little older, is a careworn sort of woman, even less effectual than her husband, Ted

Guy (*singing*)   While the moon her watch is keeping,
                    All through the night,
                 While the weary world is sleeping,
                    All through the night.

Dafydd (*over this, as Guy sings*) Good, good. Don't hunch. Don't hunch. You can't sing if you're hunched, Mr Jones. Good. (*Joining in with him, singing*) "All through the night".

Linda Washbrook and Crispin Usher have meantime entered. Linda is the nicely brought-up, rather petulant daughter of her over-anxious parents, Ted and Enid. Crispin, her currently unsuitable boyfriend, is a tough, hostile young man very much at odds with his present environment and with most of the Society

Guy (*singing*)   O'er my bosom gently stealing,
                      Visions of delight revealing,
                      Breathes a pure and holy feeling,
                      All through the night.

As he reaches the final stages of the song, Ian Hubbard and Rebecca Huntley-Pike appear. They are followed by Bridget. Ian, Fay's husband, is almost her male counterpart. An ambitious young man with a cultivated laid-back cool, designed to make money and charm women in that order. Rebecca, Jarvis's wife, is younger than him by a few years. She has that dignified appearance of one who has just had several stiff drinks. Maybe she has

Dafydd (*as Guy finishes; applauding*) Bravo. Bravo.

The rest of the company join in his applause. Guy jumps in alarm, unaware that such a large audience had gathered

Ah, here they all are. Ladies and gentlemen, may I present a new member of our Society. Mr Jones, who has just passed with flying colours.

A burst of general chatter and greeting

(*Through this*) Now, these are—these are a lot of different people who are going to have to introduce themselves. I can't be doing with that.

The following speeches overlap each other

Rebecca Hallo, welcome. Is he playing Matt the Mint?
Dafydd Ah, well. Maybe, maybe.
Rebecca We need a Matt the Mint. He'd be wonderful. Lovely voice.
Guy (*smiling gratefully*) Thank you.
Rebecca Isn't it? A lovely voice. Most unusual.
Fay Yes.
Rebecca Mr Jones, is it?
Guy Guy.
Rebecca Guy. Oh, that's a nice name. I like the name Guy, don't you? It's very masculine.
Enid Manly, yes. Manly.
Fay Frightfully, yes.
Ian Are we going on or going home? I'm for going home.
Jarvis I don't care what we do. Five past ten, I'm in the pub. I tell you.
Dafydd Everybody, could I have your attention? Please. Just a second, everybody.
Bridget (*shouting*) Shut up!
Rebecca I do wish she wouldn't shout like that.
Dafydd Now, everybody, I must apolo—
Rebecca Why can't she just ask people to be quiet?
Dafydd I must apologize, ladies and gentlemen, for making much, much slower progress than I anticipated. So, apologies for calling you all in and for keeping you hanging around. Mind you, I must say this evening has not been wasted. We've done some good solid groundwork and that's

surely going to pay off later. So what I'd like to do just before we call it a night, is a quick recap from the top. OK? All right, Ted?

Ted From the top?

Dafydd If you'd be so kind. OK, Mr Ames?

Rebecca Oh, good. We can watch.

Ted (*to Mr Ames*) We're going from the top apparently.

Mr Ames Right.

Jarvis What's the time, then?

Ian We've got half an hour yet.

Fay (*to Rebecca*) Do you want to go over now?

Rebecca Not on your life. We've all been sitting back there in the cold for two and a half hours. Let's see what they've been up to, for heaven's sake.

Dafydd So. The house lights dim. Black-out. Mr Ames in position. Ted in position. And then the soft glow of lamp light very gently—and—cue.

Mr Ames (*reading as The Beggar*) If poverty be a title to poetry, I am sure nobody can dispute mine. I own myself of the Company of Beggars; and I make one at their weekly festivals at St Giles. I have a small yearly salary for my catches, and am welcome to dinner there whenever I please, which is more than most poets can say.

Ted (*reading as Player*) As we believe by the muses, 'tis but gratitude in us to encourage poetical merit wherever we find it. Be the author who he will, we push his play as far as it will go. So (though you are in want) I wish you success heartily. But I see 'tis time for us to withdraw; the actors are preparing to begin. Play away the Overture.

Ted exits with a flourish. Then reappears somewhat sheepishly having evidently gone off the wrong way. He tiptoes across to the correct exit and, with an apologetic look at Dafydd, goes

A silence

Dafydd (*choosing to ignore Ted's mistake*) Splendid, splendid. Well done.

Rebecca Is that it?

Dafydd Yes, yes. So far.

Rebecca That's all you've done?

Dafydd Yes.

Rebecca My God. We're not on till page thirty. When do you want us? Next June?

Dafydd All right, all right.

Ted (*anxiously*) Was that OK?

Dafydd Marvellous, Ted, marvellous.

Rebecca Riveting. Can't wait to find out who done it. Right, let's have that drink, then.

A general move to the door. Chatter

Bridget exits backstage

Jarvis (*confidentially to Dafydd*) Just looking at that scene, I think you'll find it might benefit from a bit of gesture, you know . . .

Dafydd (*gathering up his things*) Yes, yes, thank you, Jarvis. I'm sure it would . . .

Jarvis It's just in those days they used their arms a lot, you know. Great deal of gesture.

Dafydd Yes, well, I'll be stuffing it full of gestures at a later stage, Jarvis. Be patient. You won't see the stage for arm movements . . .

Jarvis You don't mind me saying . . .?

Dafydd Not at all. It's just, you know with Ted you can't go too fast. It takes a month or two just to get him pointing the right way . . . You know old Ted. (*He laughs*)

Jarvis (*going out*) You don't mind me coming up with the odd idea, do you, now and again?

Dafydd Not at all, Jarvis, any time . . . feel free . . .

Jarvis goes out

(*Calling*) You really must do a production yourself sometime. (*Muttering*) And I'll come and bugger yours up, you interfering old fascist . . . (*Seeing Guy is still there*) Ah, Mr Jones, you're still here. Splendid. Fancy a quick pint? We usually go across the road to *The Fleece*. He's a cantankerous old bastard, the chap who runs it, but it's the best pint for thirty miles . . .

Guy Righto. Splendid. Lead on.

Bridget comes from backstage

Dafydd Ah, Bridget. You'll switch off, will you?

Bridget Yes.

Dafydd Bridget's our stage manager. Also playing Jenny Diver. We couldn't function at all without Bridget. She's the one who keeps us all sane, Mr Jones.

Guy Good for you. (*He smiles at Bridget*)

Bridget doesn't react. Dafydd gathers together his papers. Guy perseveres cheerily

I'm just going over the road to brave this cantankerous old publican. See you over there, perhaps.

Dafydd You certainly will. Bridget's his daughter.

Guy Ah.

Bridget Are we picking it up tomorrow from where we stopped?

Dafydd Yes, we'll carry straight on, my love.

Bridget Right. From the bottom of page one then.

Dafydd Oh, now please, please. Don't you start, there's a dear. (*To Guy*) Fit then, are you, Mr Jones? Right. Away we go.

The scene changes to the pub. A crowded saloon bar containing most of the Society. Rebecca, Enid and Fay are sitting together at one of the tables

Dafydd and Guy jostle their way in

(*Shouting above the din*) Tends to get a bit crowded but it's worth it for the beer.

Ian (*calling across*) Pint, Daf?

Dafydd Oh, bless you, my love. Though I think it's my shout.

Ian It's all right, I'm getting them.

Dafydd Pint for you, Mr Jones?

Guy Would it be all right to have a gin and tonic?

Dafydd Gin and tonic? That's what they're drinking in Leeds, is it? Right. (*Calling*) Ian? Can you get this fellow a gin and tonic?

Ian Gin and tonic. Is he coming in here a lot, is he?

Dafydd (*laughing, to Guy*) You mustn't mind him. He's got a great sense of humour. Ian and his brother, they're in partnership together. The brother does the work. Ian spends the money. (*He laughs*)

Rebecca (*her voice ringing across the pub, to Guy*) We've all voted for you to play Matt the Mint. We think you're lovely.

Guy Thank you.

Dafydd Mrs Huntley-Pike. Another singer we put well to the back. In her case preferably in the car park.

Guy Like me, you mean? (*He laughs*)

Dafydd God, no. You haven't heard her. If she sang in the dairy she'd make cheese. I tell you. Married, of course, to old Councillor Huntley-Potty-Pike. One of the whizz kids on our Council. Which explains why this town's in the state it is.

Ian (*arriving with the drinks*) There you go.

Dafydd Ah, thank you, Ian. Bless you.

Ian Gin and tonic.

Guy Thank you very much.

Ian Hope you don't want ice because he hasn't got any.

Dafydd He's got ice, the miserable old sod. He just hides it. You can't charge for it, don't put it out. That's his maxim. His beer mats are screwed to the bar. Cheers.

Ian Cheers.

Guy Here's to the—production.

Dafydd Yes, why not? Here's to it. *The Beggar's Opera*. (*Waving his glass in the direction of the women's table*) To *The Beggar's Opera*.

Fay (*echoing*) Yes. *The Beggar's Opera*.

Rebecca Hear, hear. *The Beggar's Opera*.

Guy When do we—when does it—start? Open?

A phone rings faintly from behind the bar

Dafydd Oh, not till May. We've got three and half months yet. Still, with dear old Ted there, I think we're going to need it. Mind you, we've got used to him now, haven't we, Ian? We had him one time in, what was it, *Sound of Music*, was it?—

Bridget appears the other side of the bar and calls and waves in an attempt to attract Dafydd's attention

Bridget (*calling*) Dafydd. Dafydd.

Ian (*seeing her, to Dafydd*) Dafydd, I think she wants you.

Dafydd (*turning*) Hallo. Yes, my love?

Bridget (*miming*) Phone. Phone.

Dafydd Ah. Telephone. Do excuse me, won't you? (*To Guy, handing him his*

pint) Hang on to that a second, would you mind?
Guy (*taking it*) Certainly.
Dafydd (*moving away*) I trust you.
Bridget It's Hannah for you.
Dafydd What the hell's she want . . .

Dafydd goes to a corner of the bar, takes the receiver, sticks a finger in his ear and starts a conversation which we cannot hear. With the departure of Dafydd, the small talk between Ian and Guy seems thin on the ground

Ian Cheers.
Guy Cheers.

Pause. Guy, rather nervously, takes a swig of beer

Ian Get on well with Dafydd, do you?
Guy Well, yes, I think—
Ian I hope so because you're drinking his beer.
Guy Oh, God, yes. Sorry. Do you know that's something that I'm always
 . . . well, not always— but occasionally—

Fay approaches them and interrupts

Fay Darling, have you got a light? They're all dreary non-smokers over
 there. (*Smiling at Guy, the reason for her joining them*) Hallo, I'm Fay.
 I'm this thing's wife. How do you do?
Guy Hallo.
Fay You don't know what a pleasure it is to see a new man in the Society.
 It's mostly filled with us boring women. Dreadful.
Guy (*gallantly*) Dreadful for some perhaps.
Fay (*throwing her head back with a tinkling laugh*) Yes. Depends on your
 point of view.
Ian (*not quite to himself*) Jesus . . . (*He moves away to put his glass on the
 bar*)
Fay (*after him*) Where are you off to?
Ian Going to bring the car round, why?
Fay Heavens and not yet closing time. What's come over over him? (*She
 smiles at Guy again*) Hallo.
Guy (*a fraction uneasily*) Hallo. Well, I suppose I must be making a move,
 too.
Fay You got a car? Only otherwise we could drop you.
Guy No, thanks. I'm mobile . . .

Jarvis heads towards Fay and Guy with some empty glasses

Jarvis I say, I say.
Fay (*under her breath*) Oh, no. Quick, hide, take cover.
Jarvis (*reaching them*) I say. Yes. You. You're a Scotchman, aren't you?
Guy No, no.
Jarvis They're the only people who do that, you know. The Scotties. That's
 the way you tell 'em.
Fay Tell what?

Jarvis Look, look, look. Look, you see. Glass in each hand. Whisky, beer. Whisky, beer. That's the way they do it. Scotty, right?
Guy No.
Jarvis Always tell 'em. Always tell 'em. (*He moves away*)
Guy I didn't understand that at all.
Fay (*laughing*) Don't worry. He's completely mad.
Guy Ah.
Fay Quite harmless though.
Guy Glad to hear it.
Fay No, it's her you've got to watch. (*She nods towards Rebecca*) Hallo. (*She smiles again at Guy*)

Ian returns from the bar en route *to the door. He drags Fay out with him*

(*As she's whisked away*) I think this means we're going. Goodnight, then.
Guy Goodnight.
Ian 'Night.
Fay Do excuse us. Some nights he can hardly contain himself.

Fay and Ian go out

Jarvis (*from the bar, calling to Guy*) Hey! I say, you Jimmy . . . Jimmy.
Guy (*mystified*) Me?
Jarvis You want another wee dram in there . . .
Guy No thank you, this is gin . . .
Jarvis (*to Bridget*) And a wee one for our friend from over the border.
Guy Oh, Lord . . .

Over in the other corner of the bar, Mr Ames begins playing the piano. Shortly, Ted starts singing and is then joined by most of the others

Ted (*singing*)	Fill ev'ry glass, for wine inspires us,
	And fires us
	With courage, love and joy.
All	Fill ev'ry glass, for wine inspires us,
	And fires us
	With courage, love and joy.
Ted	Women and wine should life employ.
	Is there ought else on earth desirous?
	Fill ev'ry glass, for wine inspires us,
	And fires us
	With courage, love and joy.
All	Women and wine should Life employ and etc.

Guy stands bemusedly as this starts. His bemusement slightly increases as Jarvis passes him and pours a large scotch into his gin glass. Jarvis moves to the piano and joins the singers. Dafydd, having finished on the phone, rejoins Guy

Dafydd (*over the singing*) Good old Ted. Get him near a piano, he's away. Marvellous music, isn't it? All traditional tunes, you know. All the tunes Gay used were traditional.

Guy Really?

Dafydd Still as fresh as they ever were . . .

Bridget, from the other side of the bar, appears ringing a large bell. The singing stops

Bridget My Dad says he's not licensed for music and dancing and would you please stop that bloody row . . .

A chorus of booing and catcalls

Only he didn't say please, like I did.

Crispin Why's he got a piano for, then?

Bridget That's reserved for private functions . . .

Rebecca This is a private function . . .

Crispin Yes. Bugger off . . .

Bridget Hey, you? Watch your language, you. You're not in the gutter now, you know . . .

Jarvis (*to Mr Ames*) Play a Highland Fling for the Scottie over there . . .

Bridget Sorry. Those are the rules of the house. Thank you very much. And last orders, please . . .

Crispin You want to get rid of that piano, if people can't use it . . .

Bridget (*ignoring this*) Last orders, please.

Linda It's a filthy place anyway.

Bridget You know where to go if you don't like it, don't you? Sitting there drinking half of shandy for three hours, we can do without you for a kick off . . .

Linda What's it got to do with you what I drink? What on earth business is it of yours, may I ask . . .

Bridget (*mimicking her*) What on earth business is it of yours, may I ask?

Dafydd All right, girls, that's enough now . . . Call a truce.

Linda Snotty little barmaid . . .

Ted Now, now, Linda . . .

Bridget (*looking dangerous*) Hey . . . hey . . . You watch yourself.

Enid Now come on, Linda, we're off home now . . .

Dafydd That's enough . . .

Ted Now, now, now . . . Linda . . .

Crispin plays a provocative chord on the piano

Bridget Hey, you. Did you play that? You touch that piano again, you're out that door, all right . . .

Crispin Yes, miss . . . Wasn't me, miss . . .

Linda plonks out several notes on the piano

Enid Linda! Oh, she is a naughty girl . . .

Ted Now, now, now, Linda. Now, now . . .

Bridget (*coming round the bar like a tornado*) All right, you. I've had it up to here with you . . .

Dafydd Bridget. Easy, Bridget girl. (*To Guy*) God, she doesn't want to get her roused. That girl set up *Carousel* single handed . . .

Bridge approaches Linda

Bridget Come on. Out I said.

Linda Really? You try and make me leave.

Bridget (*shoving her*) Out. Out . . .

Rebecca ⎫   Peace, children . . .
Enid   ⎪ (*together*)   Stop them somebody. Someone stop them . . .
Ted   ⎬   Now, now, Linda. Now, now . . .
Dafydd ⎭   I think we've all had our bit of fun and high spirits,
                                    people . . .

Crispin, during this last, steps between Bridget and Linda and confronts Bridget

Crispin Hey . . . Who you pushing around then?

Bridget Anyone who gets in my way. Want to make something of it?

Crispin Haven't you ever heard that the customer's always right? Haven't you ever heard that, then?

Bridget Not in this pub they aren't. Now sod off . . .

Crispin Language, language . . . (*He pats her under the chin*)

Bridget really goes wild, launching herself at Crispin with an initial knee to the groin which he narrowly avoids. She follows this with a huge swinging punch, which again, he narrowly avoids and which—had it connected—would certainly have laid him out cold. Under this barrage of kicks and punches, Crispin beats a somewhat undignified retreat towards the door. Linda watches appalled. The others respond with a mixture of amusement and alarm

Bridget (*as this happens*) Go on . . . get out, out, out, out, OUT!

Crispin (*half amused at this onslaught*) All right, all right, all right. I'm going. I'm going.

Crispin and Bridget both disappear into the street momentarily. Then Bridget returns triumphantly. She gets a cheer

Linda stalks with dignity to the door. Bridget, with mock politeness, holds open the door for her

Enid (*apprehensively*) Linda . . .

Linda (*coolly*) Good night.

Bridget Good nate.

Linda goes out

And it is now time, please, so can I have your glasses? Thank you.

Mutters and groans of complaint

Jarvis (*calling to Guy*) Hey! Scottie. Remind you of Glasgow, eh? Home from home. (*He laughs*)

Dafydd (*gloomily*) Whenever you're in here you just have to keep saying over to yourself, "I know it's hell but the beer is good." That my glass, is it?

Guy (*handing him the totally depleted glass*) Yes. Sorry.

Dafydd Oh, well. Bang goes another reason for living. (*He shrugs*) I hope
Bridget hasn't offended that lad. We need him for the show.
Guy What's he playing?
Dafydd Macheath. Well, maybe he wasn't the most ideal choice for the
leading role. Temperamentally, anyway. But we had no real choice. Not
with Tommy Binns' cartilage problem.

Rebecca and Jarvis pass them on their way out, Rebecca moving with extreme,
sedate caution

Dafydd Goodnight, both.
Rebecca Goodnight. (*With a glassily charming smile to Guy*) See you
tomorrow.
Guy Yes, indeed ...
Jarvis See you the noo. Eh? See you the noo ... (*He laughs*)
Guy (*laughing*) Yes, yes ...
Rebecca (*as they go out*) Are you sure he's Scottish ...?

Rebecca and Jarvis leave

Dafydd See you where did he say?
Guy The noo.
Dafydd It's just round the back. (*He roars with laughter and slaps Guy on the*
shoulder) Sorry, Guy, you'll have to bear with my coarse Welsh rugby
player's humour. ... Beg your pardon.
Guy Are you a rugger player?
Dafydd God, no. Can't stand the game. Had to play it for seven years.
Total misery. But my Dad was a fanatic. One of those. All his language
was in terms of rugby, you know. That man's up and under imagery
constituted my entire verbal childhood upbringing. Making sure life fed
you plenty of good clean ball. Getting women in loose mauls and all that
bollocks. God, I was glad to leave home ...
Guy Your poor mother ...
Dafydd No, she was all right, she left with me ...

Ted and Enid pass them

Goodnight, Ted. Enid ...
Enid We're going off in search of Linda, Dafydd ...
Ted She's only a child you see, Dafydd ...
Enid (*almost overlapping him*) She's always been mature, you know ...
Ted (*almost overlapping her, in turn*) ... physically, you know ...
Enid ... physically ... but emotionally ...
Ted ... her emotions are still very far from ...
Enid ... for her age ...
Ted ... mature, you see.
Enid ... immature, yes.
Ted And we're not happy with this lad at all, Dafydd. I mean we're not ...
Enid ... snobbish at all ...
Ted ... class conscious. But he's not right ...
Enid ... he's very wrong ...

Ted ... he's a very wild lad ...
Enid ... oh, very wild ...
Ted ... and we've got a feeling we know where he'll finish up, don't we, Enid?
Enid Yes, I'm afraid we do. Only too ...
Ted ... too well ...
Enid ... too well ...

They both mercifully run out of steam. Slight pause

Dafydd Well. If you find you do have a problem, give me a ring at home.
Ted Thank you, Dafydd ...
Enid Thank you very much, Dafydd ...
Dafydd I'll be back there in ten minutes. So. 'Night.
Ted Goodnight.
Enid Goodnight. I hope you sleep well. (*To Guy*) All through the night. (*She laughs*)
Guy Thank you. Goodnight. (*He laughs*)

Ted and Enid go out

Dafydd An effortlessly witty woman is Enid, you'll discover. Listen, we haven't settled this business of casting, have we? Think we ought to settle that now, don't you?
Guy Yes. That would be nice. Give me something to be getting on with. If I know what I'm playing ...
Bridget (*making a threatening move to come round the bar*) Are you two leaving or do I have to throw you out?
Dafydd (*retreating in haste*) No, no, Bridget. We're going. We're going. Have you got your car, by any chance ...?
Guy Yes. Just round the corner ...
Dafydd Well, look my place is only a couple of streets away. I could give you a script and a cup of cocoa. That suit you?
Guy Fine. Lead on.

Guy and Dafydd leave the pub

Bridget continues to clear up for a moment

Suddenly, Crispin is in the doorway. He stands menacingly

Bridget sees him and tenses, ready for a scrap. Silence. Crispin advances on her slowly. They stand face to face. With a sudden swift movement he reaches out and grabs her by the back of her head. Their mouths meet in a savage kiss

The scene changes to Dafydd's sitting-room. Pleasant and comfortable but small. Certainly too small for Dafydd. A room shared with children. A large, male, home-made rag doll sits on one of the chairs

Dafydd (*in a whisper*) Yes ... As I thought. She'll be in bed. She's not much of a night owl, my wife. Of course the children get her up pretty early ...
Guy How many do you have?
Dafydd Two. Twin girls.

Guy (*indicating the doll*) Is that theirs?

Dafydd Oh yes—let me take your coat—he's what they call their Other Daddy. Whenever I'm away, they bring him out and pretend it's me. I think it's been left there as a hint by someone this evening. I'll put the kettle on. Won't be a second. If you're cold at all, put the fire on. Personally, I think it's pretty warm, don't you? Wait there . . .

Dafydd exits

Guy surveys the room. After a moment, he sits and waits patiently. It's obviously quite chilly

> *Quite suddenly and unexpectedly, Hannah enters. She is in her night things, her face shiny with cream and she is obviously not expecting company*

Hannah (*speaking as she enters*) Dafydd, if you want anything to—(*She sees Guy*) Oh.

Guy (*rising*) Hallo, I'm—

Hannah Oh, God. Excuse me.

> *Hannah flees the room*

Guy stands a little bemused. The following conversation is heard off

Hannah (*off*) Dafydd . . .

Dafydd (*off, cheerfully*) Hallo, darling. Got a little bit held up, sorry.

Hannah (*off*) You told me you weren't bringing anyone home.

Dafydd (*off*) Yes, I know, I know.

Hannah (*off*) I mean I phoned especially, Dafydd. I phoned and said would you be bringing any of them home tonight . . .

Dafydd (*off, under her*) It was a spur of the moment decision . . .

Hannah (*off*) . . . and you said no which is why I got ready for bed.

Dafydd (*off*) You can go to bed. You can go to bed.

Hannah (*off*) Not if there's someone here I can't.

Dafydd (*off*) It's all right. This chap doesn't matter.

Hannah (*off*) Who is he?

Dafydd (*off*) He's no one. He's no one important. He's a small part player, that's all.

Hannah (*off*) I'll get dressed.

Dafydd (*off, calling after her as she departs*) Don't bother. He's not worth getting dressed for. (*Pause*) God damn it.

A door slams off

> *A second later, Dafydd reappears. He is holding a script*

Here we are. Sorry to keep you. (*He is suddenly aware that Guy must have heard some of the conversation*) Things are just—heating up out there. By the way, I never asked you. Tea, coffee or cocoa?

Guy Tea?

Dafydd No problem. Now—(*He studies the script*) I—er—hear you ran into the wife.

Guy Well . . .

Dafydd Or rather she ran into you. (*He laughs*)

Guy That's more it, yes.

Dafydd (*feeling some explanation is due but unable to think of one*) Yes. She's—you know—women . . .

Guy Yes.

Dafydd Never like being taken by surprise, do they? Unless they know what it is in advance. (*He laughs*) I'd like to surprise you for your birthday, darling, what would you like? Now then. This casting business. I have a feeling, an instinctive feeling in my bones, you know, and I'm not often wrong—sometimes, not often—that you'd make a pretty good Crook-Finger'd Jack. Fancy that, do you? Having a crack at Crook-Finger'd Jack?

Guy Yes, he sounds pretty interesting . . . yes . . .

Dafydd I'll be honest, it's not a vast—you know *The Beggar's Opera* at all—?

Guy No. It's one I haven't . . .

Dafydd No, well, it's as I say, it's not a vast part. But he does feature. He features pretty strongly really. I mean for the sort of size of part he is. I mean, he's got—what—in terms of speeches—? (*He flicks the script vaguely*) Well, he's got probably just the one line in Act Two but he's the sort of character, you know, at the end of an evening, an audience tend to remember quite graphically . . .

Guy Perhaps that's because of his finger . . .

Dafydd (*failing to see this small joke*) What? No, you see the play's full of these marvellous characters. There are the highwaymen . . . (*savouring the names*) Crook-Finger'd Jack, Jemmy Twitcher, Nimming Ned, Ben Budge, Matt of the Mint . . . (*He reflects*) Yes, there was the possibility of that character but—my feeling is, as director, that Matt of the Mint could be a little too adventurous for you first time round.

Guy No, fair enough. I wasn't . . .

Dafydd That, of course, is not in any way a reflection on . . .

Guy No, please, please. I'll be guided by you . . .

Dafydd (*relieved*) Well. Good. Good. I'm giving that particular part to Dr Packer who has, to be fair, had a good deal of experience. Still, it'll only be the first of many for you and us. Hopefully.

Guy I hope so, too.

Dafydd Good. (*He hands Guy the script*) You want to take this one?

Guy Thank you.

Dafydd You'll find he comes on around page thirty-two. Then he goes off on page thirty-five, I think. And then I'm thinking seriously about bringing him on again in Act Three. But that's to be confirmed.

Guy Splendid. Thank you very much.

Dafydd Quite a departure for PALOS, this, you know . . .

Guy PALOS?

Dafydd Pendon Amateur Light Operatic Society . . .

Guy Oh, yes. Sorry. Of course . . .

Dafydd Makes a change from *The Student Prince*. Not that I don't . . . But it's good to have a change now and again. I had a lot of opposition in Committee over this one I can tell you. Lot of old die-hards there.

Original walk-ons in *Chu Chin Chow*. You know the sort ... But I'm
absolutely convinced that this show—first produced when was it—?
1728—it's as entertaining and as vital and as relevant as it was then ...
Suky Tawdry ... Dolly Trull ... Mrs Vixen ... Those are the whores and
pimps of the town ... almost see their faces in their names, can't you?
Polly Peachum. That tells you all you need to know about her, doesn't it?
What an age, eh? What an age. Well, compared to our own.

Guy Yes. Yes. Of course, they didn't have any ...

Dafydd I mean, look at us today. Sex shops, I ask you. Can you imagine
Captain Macheath furtively purchasing marital aids ...? What's happened to us, Guy? What's happened to us, eh? (*Slight pause*) Sorry, I get a
little—over-enthusiastic occasionally. So I'm told.

Guy Not at all. Did you ever consider doing the theatre professionally? I
mean, it's just that you seem ...

Dafydd Oh, I was, I was. I was in the profession for some years.

Guy Really?

Dafydd Oh, yes. I've done my bit.

Guy As a producer?

Dafydd No, no. Acting in those days. I was acting. And a little bit of stage
management, you know.

Guy Whereabouts?

Dafydd (*vaguely*) Oh, all over. A lot of it in Minehead.

Guy Oh. Yes.

Dafydd Still. That's under the bridge. Respectable solicitor these days.
Well, reasonably. What line are you in, then?

Guy Oh, I'm—

*Before he can reply, Hannah enters. She has made herself more socially
presentable now, pretending the earlier encounter with Guy did not occur.
She carries a tray with two mugs of cocoa*

*Guy rises politely. Dafydd, unused to such niceties in his own home, does so
belatedly*

Hannah Hallo ...

Guy Hallo.

Dafydd Here she is ... This is my wife, Hannah.

Hannah How do you do?

Guy How do you do?

Dafydd Dearest, this is Mr Jones. Guy Jones.

Hannah Hallo.

Guy Hallo.

Dafydd Let me ... (*He helps her with the tray*) ... On here, shall we?

Hannah Yes, it'll mark it on there ... (*To Guy*) Do sit down, please ... Brrr!
It's cold in here. Heating's off.

Dafydd Is it? Can't say we'd noticed, had we? Boiling.

Hannah I presumed you both wanted cocoa. I saw the tin was out.

Dafydd Oh, no. Guy wanted tea. Sorry, love ...

Guy It doesn't matter ...

Hannah I can make tea ...

Guy No, please, really . . .
Dafydd Tea's no trouble . . .
Guy No, this is perfect. Please.
Hannah Well. If you're quite sure.
Guy I'm just as happy with this.

Slight pause

Hannah Well, I'll leave you both to it, then.
Dafydd Don't go, don't go . . .
Hannah If you want to talk business . . .
Dafydd No, we've finished. Sit down for a second.
Guy (*smiling*) Please.
Hannah Well. Only if I'm not in the way. (*She sits*)
Dafydd Anyway. Hardly call it business, could we?
Hannah Oh?
Dafydd Guy's going to be giving us his Crook-Finger'd Jack.
Hannah Sorry?
Dafydd Our missing brigand. He's just joined us.
Hannah Oh. Wonderful.
Dafydd Think he'll make a good Jack, do you, Hannah? Think he'll make a
   highwayman?
Hannah Well. Possibly . . .
Dafydd Oh dear, Guy. She doesn't sound too convinced. Doesn't he
   convince you?
Hannah Well. Possibly . . .
Dafydd Oh dear, Guy. She doesn't sound too convinced. Doesn't he
   convince you?
Hannah Yes. I just think he looks a bit handsome for a highwayman. (*She
   smiles nervously*)
Dafydd (*roaring with laughter*) Well, I don't know what you say to that,
   Guy, I really don't. What do you say to that?
Guy I don't really know. (*He smiles*)

Dafydd's laughter subsides. A silence

Dafydd Maybe we can give him an eyepatch.
Hannah Yes . . .

They laugh. Another silence

Dafydd Are the girls all right?
Hannah Yes. They're asleep.
Dafydd Gwinny stopped coughing?
Hannah Oh yes, I gave her the linctus.
Dafydd Good. Good. (*Pause*) Good.
Hannah (*to Guy*) We have twin girls.
Guy Yes . . .
Hannah Gwynneth who's got a cold. And Myfanwy who's just getting over
   it . . . They just go in circles.
Guy Nice names.

Hannah Yes. Dafydd's mother chose them.

Dafydd With our help.

Guy Ah ...

Dafydd Everything's Welsh in this house ...

Hannah Except me, that is.

Dafydd Except her, that is. She was made in Middlesex.

Guy (*rather over-reacting*) Oh, really? Middlesex.

Hannah Yes. Are you from Middlesex, then?

Guy No.

Hannah Oh.

Dafydd He's from Leeds. Aren't you?

Guy That's right.

Hannah Oh. Leeds, yes ... Is your wife local?

Dafydd No, dearest, he hasn't got a wife ...

Hannah No?

Guy No, she ... she died, recently.

Hannah Oh, dear.

Dafydd Oh dear, I didn't know that. Accident, was it?

Guy No. Not really it was ... (*he searches for words*)

Dafydd Deliberate. (*He laughs*)

Hannah (*fiercely*) Dafydd ...

Dafydd Sorry, sorry. I do beg your pardon. I'm sorry, Guy.

Guy That's quite all right ...

Hannah He's always doing that.

Guy She was ill for some time actually ...

Hannah Oh, dear. How long's she ... How long's she—been now?

Guy Just over a year ...

Hannah Ah.

Dafydd Ah ...

Guy It took me a little time, obviously, to adjust ...

Hannah ... yes, it would ...

Guy Still, eventually I decided it was high time I took a grip on things and got out and about again. Which is why I took the plunge and wrote to David ...

Dafydd (*correcting him*) Dafydd ...

Guy (*attempting the correct pronunciation*) Dafydd ...

Dafydd Nearly. (*He spells it out slowly*) Da—fydd ...

Guy Da—fydd ...

Hannah Oh, really. It's near enough.

Dafydd Near enough is not enough ...

Hannah It's bad enough as it is. How do you fancy standing in the dry cleaners trying to pronounce your own surname?

Dafydd (*the full Welsh*) Llewellyn. What could be simpler? Llewellyn ...

Hannah You work locally, though, do you?

Guy Yes, I'm with BLM actually.

Dafydd BLM? Over on Western Estate?

Guy That's right ...

Dafydd The big boys, eh?

Guy Well, they are, I'm not.

Hannah What do they do, BLM? I've always meant to ask.

Guy Well ...

Dafydd That's a difficult one to answer, eh, Guy?

Guy Just a bit ...

Hannah I mean, what do they do? Do they make anything?

Dafydd (*laughing*) Vast profits mostly ... Right?

Guy Right. (*He laughs*)

Hannah Oh well, don't tell me if you don't want to ...

Guy We're a multi-national company that's become extremely diversified ...

Dafydd Diversified, dearest. That means they're into all sorts of different—

Hannah (*tetchily*) Yes, I know, I know ...

Dafydd All right ...

Hannah I know what diversify means.

Guy (*a fraction embarrassed*) And so it's a bit difficult to pin down. Certainly it is from my limited viewpoint. In a rather small local branch in a rather obscure department called Alternative Forward Costing. In which I am a very small cog indeed.

Hannah I'm impressed anyway.

Dafydd It's interesting you should be in BLM because—

In the hall, the phone rings

Hannah Who can that be ...? (*She starts to rise*)

Dafydd (*rising*) I'll go, I'll go. It could be Ted ...

Hannah Oh, is it Linda trouble again?

Dafydd (*as he goes*) Yes, as usual. As usual ...

Dafydd goes out

Hannah It's these friends of ours, they have this daughter that they absolutely dote over. And of course she just takes terrible advantage of them all the time ...

Guy Yes, I met them.

Hannah Did you, yes. She's a real headache for them. She set fire to all her mother's clothes, you know ...

Guy Set fire to them?

Hannah Yes. Enid wasn't in them at the time but it was everything she had in the world except what she was standing up in. They both came home from a meeting of the Civic Society and her wardrobe was ablaze.

Guy Heavens.

Hannah Mind you, I can't help thinking, in some ways, they brought it on themselves. I hope ours will turn out all right. Do you have children, Mr—?

Guy Guy, please. No. My wife wasn't able to have any. She—wasn't very strong ...

Hannah Shame. Do you miss her a lot?

Guy (*as if considering the question for the first time*) Yes. Yes, I do. Very much.

Hannah That's nice. For her, I mean. Of course not for you. I'd like to think I'd be missed.

Guy You?

Hannah Yes.

Guy Why! (*An awful thought*) You're not . . .?

Hannah Oh, no. No, I'm right as rain. I think. So far as I know. It's just I sometimes wonder, I suppose a lot of us do probably, whether if I—you know—died people would really . . . Silly really, isn't it?

Guy I'm sure you'd be missed.

Hannah Maybe.

Guy By David—Dafydd. And your children.

Hannah Yes, possibly the children would. For a few more years, anyway. I don't know about Dafydd. Now he *is* missed. You see that big doll there? Every time Dafydd's out of the house for more than twenty minutes the girls insist it's brought out. Then all their games revolve round that wretched doll. Tea with Daddy-doll and Walks with Daddy-doll and Supper with Daddy-doll and Bed with Daddy-doll . . . Well, I've stopped them taking it to bed with them now. I did think that was getting too much of a good thing. Of course, Dafydd thinks it's terribly funny. I suppose it is quite flattering for him, really. The trouble is, my family are under the impression that there's a female counterpart to that thing that runs round the house after them. Only it happens to be me. Hooray for Mummy-doll. (*Slight pause*) Heavens. I haven't talked like this for years. I am sorry. It's very boring of me.

Guy (*gently*) No.

Hannah No?

Guy No. (*He smiles at her*)

Hannah, uncertainly at first and then more warmly, smiles back at Guy

As they gaze at each other, Dafydd returns from the phone to break the spell

Dafydd (*as he enters*) That was Enid. They got home and found Linda in bed.

Hannah is about to say something

Yes, that's what I asked. And the answer is no. Fast asleep on her own. So, false alarm. They still have a daughter and more important we still have a Lucy Lockit. What's been going on in here? Anything I should know about?

Hannah I think it's my bedtime, if you'll excuse me . . .

Guy (*looking at his watch*) Oh, Lord, yes. I must be . . .

Dafydd Don't go on my account. I'm a late one myself . . .

Guy No, it really is . . .

Dafydd I'll fetch your coat, then.

Dafydd exits

Guy (*to Hannah*) Thank you very much for your hospitality . . .

Hannah Not much of that. You didn't even drink your cocoa.

Guy Another time, perhaps.

Dafydd returns and helps Guy into his coat

Thank you. I hope, in any case, I'll see you again before too long.
Dafydd What her? You're talking about Hannah, you mean? You'll see her tomorrow night.
Guy (*pleased*) Oh, really?
Dafydd Didn't she tell you she's in the show? She's our Polly Peachum, aren't you, love? (*He cuffs her affectionately*)
Guy Oh. I see. Good Lord.
Hannah (*as she picks up the tray*) I look better in the mornings. Usually. (*She laughs*) See you tomorrow.

Hannah exits

Guy Goodnight. (*He stares after her somewhat as of a man enchanted*)
Dafydd (*a man with his mind on more serious things*) Listen, Guy . . . a word before you go . . .
Guy Yes?
Dafydd This coincidence of your working for BLM. It could be quite opportune. The point is, I'm acting for a client at the moment who's involved in purchasing a couple of acres of wasteland. Small stuff. Nothing very exciting. Except for two things. One, the land is actually slap bang adjoining your premises—
Guy Oh, round the back there, you mean?
Dafydd Yes, the old sports field. Used to be a sports field. Second, and this is only hearsay, rumour has it that you boys are shortly planning to expand. Any truth in that, do you know?
Guy No, I don't . . . Not so far as I know . . .
Dafydd Only, of course, if you are, then of course the land in question could suddenly be worth a bit. Do you follow?
Guy Yes, I do see.
Dafydd Depending of course on how many people get to know about it. I mean, putting it in plainer words, if the chap who's selling it doesn't know, whereas we who are buying it do know—then we could be getting a bargain. But you've no definite knowledge yourself?
Guy No, as I say, not that's come to my ears. I could ask . . .
Dafydd Well, tactfully if you do. Don't want to disturb things, do we? Of course, if you could help, there'd—there'd be some arrangement, no doubt . . .
Guy Oh, there'd be no need for . . .
Dafydd Oh, yes, yes. Fair's fair. Fair's fair . . .
Guy Yes. Though I suppose if we were being really fair, we really ought to warn the person who's selling the land.
Dafydd Oh, I don't think that's on.
Guy No?
Dafydd If I did that, I'd be betraying my own client, wouldn't I? Wouldn't be ethical.
Guy I see.
Dafydd No. It's up to this other fellow's solicitor to warn him. Not me.

Anyway. Keep your ear to the ground. (*He steers Guy towards the front door*)

Guy I will certainly.

Dafydd But remember, mum's the word.

Guy Oh, yes, rather. Goodnight then. See you tomorrow.

Dafydd You betcher. Seven o'clock. And we're really going to get cracking, I can tell you. You won't see that stage for dust.

Guy (*moving away*) Right ...

Guy exits

Dafydd (*calling after Guy*) Better bring your racing skates ...

Dafydd stands in the doorway for a second, savouring the night air. A man well pleased with his evening's achievements

As he stands there, the Lights come up on Ted at next evening's rehearsal in full evening dress, holding his script

Ted (*as Peachum, singing*)
>A fox may steal your hens, sir,
>A whore your health and pence, sir,
>Your daughter rob your chest, sir,
>Your wife may steal your rest, sir,
>A thief your goods and plate.
>But this is all but picking,
>With rest, pence, chest and chicken;
>It ever was decreed, sir,
>If lawyer's hand is fee'd, sir,
>He steals your whole estate.

The Lights come up on the full rehearsal area. Also on stage now are Dafydd, prowling the auditorium watching Ted. Guy sitting to one side, absorbed and eager to learn. Bridget sitting with the prompt script, slightly bored and restless. And away in another corner Ian, at present reading the evening paper and taking no perceptible interest in proceedings. As the song finishes, Ted consults his script, makes to sit, changes his mind and exits offstage. As he does so Enid, as Mrs Peachum, and Hannah, as Polly come on, also holding their scripts. Enid is also in evening dress

Hannah (*reading, as Polly*) 'Twas only Nimming Ned. He brought in a damask window-curtain, a hoop petticoat, a pair of silver candlesticks, a perriwig, and one silk stocking, from the fire that happen'd last night.

Hannah stops at the end of her speech. Both women look up expecting Ted to reply, but he has gone

Dafydd (*yelling*) Go on, go on, go on. Don't stop again, for God's sake. We're ten days behind as it is.

Hannah We can't go on.

Dafydd Who's next, Bridget? Keep your eye on the script, girl. Who speaks next?

Bridget Ted.

Dafydd Ted? Well, where the hell is Ted? He's just walked off the stage. Where's he gone to? (*Yelling*) Ted!

Ted returns a little apprehensively

Ted Did you want me, Dafydd?

Dafydd Ted, love, there is no earthly point in leaving the stage when you're in the middle of a scene, now is there?

Ted (*consulting his script*) Oh. Don't I go off? I thought I went off ...

Enid and Hannah go to Ted's rescue, showing him where he is in the script

Hannah ... I don't think you go off till there, Ted ...

Enid ... there, dear, you see. Not till there ...

Ted ... Oh, I see. There. I thought it was there ...

Dafydd (*on the move; with impatience to Guy, over this last*) Unbelievable this, isn't it? Unbelievable. Ten days we've been at this. Ten days. And where are we—? Page fifteen or something ...

Hannah (*to Dafydd*) We've got it, now. It was a mistake.

Ted My mistake. Sorry, everyone. I shouldn't have gone off ...

Dafydd Well, I'm sure you were only expressing in actions, Ted, what will, by this stage, be the heartfelt wish of the entire audience ...

Ted (*laughing, nervously*) Yes, yes ...

Dafydd Those that won't already have dozed off, or died of old age ...

Hannah (*in a warning tone*) Dafydd ...

Dafydd Why are you dressed like a cinema manager, anyway, Ted?

Hannah It's their dinner dance, Dafydd. They were due there an hour ago. You promised to release them early.

Dafydd Oh, terrific. My whole rehearsal grinds to a halt because of a Co-op staff dance, does it?

Ted No hurry, Dafydd. No hurry. We didn't want the dinner.

Dafydd All right. Let's get on. (*Fiercely*) On, on ...

Hannah (*picking it up again, as Polly*) ... one silk stocking, from the fire that happen'd last night.

Ted (*as Peachum*) There is not a fellow that is cleverer in his way, and saves more goods out of the ...

Bridget That's cut.

Ted Sorry?

Enid I think we cut that, dear ...

Dafydd (*storming on to the stage*) Ted, that is cut. That was cut two days ago ...

Ted I'm sorry. I didn't have it ...

Dafydd You don't have anything, Ted. That's your trouble, man. You don't have any ability, you don't have any intelligence, you don't have one single scrap of artistic sensibility and most important of all you don't even have a bloody pencil.

Hannah Dafydd ...

Dafydd (*wrenching Ted's script from his hands*) *That* is cut ... (*Stabbing his finger at the page*) *That* is cut and *that* is cut. And the whole— (*wrestling with the script*)—sodding thing is cut. (*He rips Ted's script in several* *pieces. Breathlessly*) There! That make it any easier for you? You boneheaded—tortoise . . .

Ted stands shattered. He opens his mouth to reply and finds himself unable to do so

> *Ted leaves the stage rather swiftly, one suspects on the verge of tears*

Enid Oh, Dafydd . . . You really are—sometimes. You really are . . . There was no need for that . . .

> *Enid goes off after Ted*

Dafydd God, it's hot in here, isn't it? Anybody else find it too hot?

Hannah (*in a low voice*) That was unforgivable, Dafydd. To Ted of all people. Absolutely unforgivable . . . (*She picks up the torn script. Shouting angrily*) And these scripts are supposed to go back. I hope you realize that.

> *Hannah goes off after Ted and Enid*

Dafydd (*searching for fresh allies*) Dear old Guy. Dear old Guy. You sitting there quietly picking up some tips, are you?

Guy (*smiling*) Yes, yes . . .

Dafydd I'm afraid this is what we term the amateur syndrome, Guy. When the crunch comes, they can't take the pressure, you see. Want to be off to their dinner dances. God, there are times when I come close to wishing I was back at Minehead.

Guy I wondered—if you had a minute—I wondered if I could ask you about Crook-Finger'd Jack . . .

Dafydd Who?

Guy My part. Crook-Finger'd Jack . . .

Dafydd Oh, Crook-Finger'd Jack. Yes. What about him?

Guy It's just that I've been thinking about it over the past few days, you know, and I wondered whether you'd like him with a finger.

Dafydd A what?

Guy A finger. (*He holds up his hand and demonstrates a crooked finger*) Something like that.

> *Pause*

Or maybe—the other hand. (*He changes hands*)

> *Pause*

(*Offering Dafydd an alternating choice of hands*) Which do you think?

Dafydd (*snapping out of his reverie*) Yes. Do you think we could leave that for a day or two longer, Guy, old boy? I've one or two rather more pressing matters . . .

Guy Oh yes, yes. Of course. Sorry.

Bridget I'm going to make some tea. (*She starts to get up slowly*)

Dafydd Splendid, my love, excellent . . .

> *Rebecca and Fay come on, followed by Linda. All are wearing coats. Bridget exits*

Rebecca Dafydd. We come to you as a deputation. We have been sitting backstage in that ghastly smelly little kitchen for the best part of two weeks ...

Dafydd All right, all right, all right. Don't you start ...

Rebecca We're not being unreasonable, Dafydd. All we want to know is, will you be needing us this evening or will you not? If not, fair enough. Only some of us have nice, comfy homes we'd prefer to be in ...

Dafydd Go on, go home. Go home to your nice, comfy little homes. Go on, bugger off, the lot of you.

A glacial moment

Rebecca Well, I am certainly not staying after that. Not to listen to language like that.

Dafydd Goodbye.

Rebecca And furthermore, I shall be having a word with the Committee about this whole business. Do you realize Mr Washbrook is in tears out there?

Dafydd So am I ...

Rebecca (*to Fay*) Are you coming, Fay?

Fay No point in staying here, is there?

    Rebecca sweeps out

Fay goes to follow. Guy watches her

    (*To Ian, indicating Guy*) We're going over the road, all right?

Ian Right. (*He starts to fold up his paper*)

Fay (*to Guy, brightly, knowing he is watching her*) You coming for a drink?

Guy Probably. In a minute.

Fay Good. See you over there.

    Fay goes out after Rebecca

Linda moves to follow them

    Bridget returns with a pint of milk

Dafydd Linda, is your Crispin around anywhere, do you know?

Linda I don't know where he is. Why should I know?

Dafydd Well, have you seen him?

Linda No, I have not seen him and I have no wish to see him, thank you very much ... (*At Bridget*) I should ask her.

Dafydd Oh, God. (*To Bridget*) Do you know where he is?

Bridget Where I left him probably.

Dafydd Where.

Bridget In my bed. Asleep.

    Linda glares furiously and goes. Bridget goes out, looking pleased. She passes Ted and Enid, now in their coats, who both cross the stage on their way out. Both are very tearful and snuffling softly

Dafydd watches them go

Dafydd (*rather lamely*) Goodnight ... folks. Have a great—evening, won't you? (*After they've gone; filled with remorse*) Oh, God. (*He sits*)

Almost immediately, Hannah returns

Hannah I told the Washbrooks they could go. Phone for you, backstage. Dr Packer. Says it's urgent.

Dafydd More problems ... more problems ...

Dafydd exits

Hannah catches Guy's eye briefly and smiles. Ian intercepts the look

Hannah goes after Dafydd

Ian moves to the door

Ian Right. After that exhausting night's work, I feel like some refreshment. (*To Guy*) You coming?

Guy I was just going to run my line a couple of times. I've got one or two ideas I'd like to try ...

Ian (*dryly*) Well, don't get stale, will you? Two months to go yet. (*He starts to move off*)

Guy (*calling him back*) I say ... (*He demonstrates his Crook-Finger'd Jack stance again*) Do you think this is too obvious? Crook-Finger'd Jack ...

Ian Can't be too obvious for Dafydd. Did you see his *Sound of Music*?

Guy No.

Ian He had them all on trampolines.

Guy Heavens.

Ian Bloody hills were alive, I can tell you. So were the front stalls. Once they got in their costumes they couldn't control the bounce, you see. Screaming nuns crashing down on the punters. Three broken legs and one of them concussed on the spot bar. Probably some still up there for all we know ...

Guy (*not knowing quite whether to believe this*) Yes. I think I'll try it without the finger to start with ...

Ian By the way ...?

Guy Mm?

Ian We'd like to invite you round some evening. To our place.

Guy Oh. That's very nice. Thank you.

Ian I don't know if you've got anyone you'd care to bring. I understand you're not married any more ...

Guy No, my wife was—

Ian Yes. Well. I daresay you've got a friend. Or someone. Eh?

Guy Yes, I think I could probably find a friend, yes.

Ian (*smiling*) Female, of course.

Guy Oh yes. Of course. Don't want to spoil your numbers.

Ian No, no. (*Pause. Uncertain whether Guy has got the message*) The point is Fay and I, we—well, you've probably gathered by now she's pretty— gregarious.

Guy Yes.

Ian And. She likes to meet new people. All the time. And frankly, so do I. So it all tends to work out. If you follow me.

Guy (*who doesn't*) Well, that's splendid. When were you thinking?

Ian Is Friday OK for you?

Guy Friday, yes.

Ian We can have a bit of fun. (*He laughs*)

Guy Splendid.

Ian Don't forget your friend, though.

Guy I won't.

Ian (*as he leaves*) And I'd like to talk to you about your job sometime. I'm very interested in that.

Ian goes

Guy (*puzzled*) Really? (*Realizing he is alone, he decides to experiment. As Jack*) "Where shall we find such another set . . ." (*He breaks off*) No. (*Trying again*) "Where shall we find such another set of practical philosophers who to a man are above the fear of death? Ha! Ha! Ho." (*He tries again*)

Jarvis enters from backstage, on his way home. He watches Guy

Guy stops, rather embarrassed as he becomes aware of Jarvis

Jarvis Hey! The noo. That's what I like to see. A man practising his craft. I have a story about that. Will interest you. When I first went into 't firm as an apprentice lad—no matter I were boss's son I started on 't shop floor—the first day there the foreman says—big fellow he was—sweep that floor spotless, lad. Spotless. I want to eat my dinner off that floor. All right? And I sort of half-swept it, you know, like you might. And when he comes back he said, what's this then, he says? And he bends down and he picks up this handful of sawdust that I'd missed, like. Under the bench. And he says, you're not expecting me to eat me dinner off this floor then, are you? He says, I'd like to see you try it, my lad, he says. And he tells me, sit down, and he fetches a gummy-bowl and spoon from rack and he makes me eat all that sawdust. Just as it is. Every scrap.

Guy Heavens.

Jarvis Nothing on it. Nor milk nor sugar. Raw sawdust. And it's the same like that every day for three months. No matter I were 't boss's son. Those lads down in that shop, they taught me the hard way with mouthfuls of sawdust.

Guy Tough life.

Jarvis Oh, aye. Mind you, a while later, me Dad had his stroke and I took over 't firm. I went down that shop, first thing I did, and sacked every bloody one of 'em. But I learnt the trade. I were grateful to 'em for that.

Guy Jolly good.

Jarvis Keep at it. Practise your gestures. They all had gestures, you know . . .

Guy I will, I will.

Jarvis An another thing. Don't put on that fancy voice for it. Use your natural accent. That's what I do. Besides, he could be a Scotty. Couldn't he? A Scotty.

Guy True, only . . .

Jarvis Stick up for thissen then, lad. Stick up for thissen. People won't think the less of you for it, you know.
Guy Yes. Right. Thank you.

Jarvis exits

Guy briefly tries his role with a thick Scots accent. More for his own amusement than anything

Wherrr shall we find such anotherrr wee set o' practical phullussupherrs. Jummy. Whoo to a man are above the ferr of dea' ...

Hannah comes on with two cups of tea. She catches some of his performance

Hannah I brought you some tea.
Guy Oh, thank you.
Hannah Dafydd's on the phone. Another crisis, I think.
Guy Ah, well.
Hannah You—er--you weren't thinking of playing him like that, were you? With that funny accent?
Guy No, no. That was just an—experiment.
Hannah Oh, good. Only I thought you nearly had it right yesterday. With the limp. The slight one.
Guy Yes. Maybe I'll stick to that. I think it's waiting all this time to rehearse the scene, it makes you—anxious ...
Hannah Yes. He'll get to you eventually.
Guy Oh, yes, I'm sure.
Hannah (*more to herself*) God knows when, though. (*She produces her script*) I wondered if you'd mind awfully hearing my lines again.
Guy No. Not at all. (*He takes her script*) Where would you ...?
Hannah Just from the top of the page.
Guy OK.
Hannah (*as Polly*) And are *you* as fond as ever, my dear?
Guy (*reading, as Macheath*) Suspect my honour, my courage, suspect any thing but my love. May my pistols miss fire, and my mare slip her shoulder while I am pursu'd, if I ever forsake thee!
Hannah (*as Polly*) Nay, my dear, I have no reason to doubt you, for I find in the romance you lent me ... (*she hesitates*)

Guy nods encouragingly

... you lent me, none of the great heroes was ever false in love.

She smiles at Guy. Guy smiles at her

Dafydd enters. His head is bowed

Hannah and Guy wrench their attention away from each other. Dafydd solemnly beats his head against a piece of furniture

Hannah (*to Dafydd*) Problems?
Dafydd One or two. Dr Packer has just phoned to inform me that faced as he is with the alternative of either reorganizing the new hospital rostas entirely or relinquishing the role of Matt of the Mint, he has reluctantly

decided on the latter course of action. So there you are. Once again, as
father would put it, we are beaten by the bounce.

Hannah What are you going to do?

Dafydd How the hell should I know?

Hannah (*softly, nodding in Guy's direction*) Guy ...

Dafydd (*sotto*) What?

Hannah Guy.

Dafydd Guy?

Hannah Yes.

Dafydd You think so?

Hannah Of course.

Dafydd (*turning to Guy, extending a hand*) Guy ...

Guy Yes?

Dafydd I think you are to be cast in the role of saviour. Can you do it? Matt
of the Mint?

Guy Oh.

Dafydd For me? For us all?

Guy Well. I'll have a go.

Dafydd Thank you. Thank you.

Hannah Super.

Dafydd (*brightening*) Splendid. Well, what do you say? A drink to cele-
brate?

Guy Well, why not?

Dafydd I'll get them in. I'll get them in. (*Moving to the door*) But tomorrow,
remember, we work ...

Guy Er ...

Dafydd Yes?

Guy What about Crook-Finger'd Jack?

Dafydd What about him?

Guy Only, I'd just learnt him. I wondered if ...

Dafydd Forget Crook-Finger'd Jack, boy. You're Matt of the Mint. You're
a star now. Nearly.

Dafydd goes

Hannah I'm so thrilled for you. Well done.

*Impetuously, she kisses him. As it turns out, it is a far more serious kiss than
either of them intended. Guy eventually releases Hannah. He moves to the
door, looking back at her. She looks at him*

Finally, Guy leaves without a further word

*As this occurs, the introduction is heard to the next song. The lights come up
on Enid, whilst also remaining on Hannah*

Enid (*as Mrs Peachum, singing*)
　　　　　　O, Polly you might have toy'd and kiss'd,
　　　　　　By keeping men off you keep them on.

Hannah (*as Polly, singing*)
　　　　　　But he so teaz'd me,

And he so pleas'd me,
What I did you must have done.
But he so teaz'ed thee/me
And he so pleas'd thee/me
What you/I did you/I must have done.

*e cross fade again and we are in Fay's sitting room. She is
le holds two exotic drinks*

Fay (*calling*) we're in here . . .
Guy (*off*) Right.
Fay (*calling*) Can you find it all right? Light switch is just inside the door.
(*She listens. Hears nothing. Assumes all is well. She puts the drinks down on
the table and checks her already faultless appearance in a mirror*)

Guy enters

Guy Sorry. At last.
Fay (*indicating his drink*) Help yourself.
Guy Thank you. (*He takes his drink*)
Fay Do tell me if it's too strong, won't you? I can never tell.
Guy (*going to drink*) No, I'm sure this will be absolutely— (*He nearly
chokes as he drinks but controls himself*)—that's—perfect, yes.
Fay Ian's just popped out. To get some more Tequila. I'm afraid we're
hooked on it these days.
Guy Oh, yes?
Fay Have you been there?
Guy Sorry?
Fay Mexico?
Guy No. No. Not Mexico . . .
Fay Glorious. Parts of it. If you dodge the poverty.
Guy Ah.
Fay So. You're the first.
Guy Yes. (*Looking round*) Yes. Looks like it.
Fay I'm all right, then, anyway.
Guy Yes?
Fay I've got you. (*She laughs*)
Guy Yes, yes. (*Pause*) I suppose that means I'm all right as well then. (*He
laughs*)
Fay (*laughing with him*) Very true, yes.

Pause

Guy (*indicating the walls*) Nice pictures.
Fay (*vaguely*) We find them quite stimulating.
Guy Yes. She's going it a bit, that one up there, isn't she?
Fay Yes. What about him behind you, then?
Guy (*turning in his chair and then with obvious shock*) Oh, good Lord. Yes.
(*Studying the picture*) Good Lord.
Fay We have to take them down when Ian's mother comes to stay . . .
Guy Yes, I can see she'd probably . . .

Fay Wait till you see what we've got in the bedroom. (*She laughs*)

Guy (*laughing inordinately*) Yes. Wow. Yes. (*Pause*) You look very nice.

Fay Thank you. So do you.

Guy (*straightening his tie*) Ah.

Fay Do you want to take that off?

Guy No, no. No. That's OK.

Fay I love men in ties ...

Guy Oh, yes? (*Pause*) You'd like it in our office then. It's full of them.

Pause

Fay Look. I might as well say this early on. Then we can relax and enjoy ourselves. If there's anything you particularly like or positively dislike, you will say, won't you?

Guy Oh no, no. I'm not at all fussy, never have been. I take just what's put in front of me.

Fay I mean, as far as I'm concerned, don't worry. I'm very easy. I don't think there's anything. Anything at all. Well, I suppose if it was excessively cruel or painful ... I would draw the line.

Guy Oh, yes, yes. (*He considers*) You mean like veal, for instance.

Fay Veal.

Guy Veal, you know ...

Fay No. I don't think I've tried that.

Guy You haven't?

Fay No. Something new. How exciting. I can't wait. Veal. How do you spell it?

Guy Er ... V-E-A-L ...

Fay You mean the same as the meat? What's it stand for?

Guy No idea ...

Fay Very Exciting And Lascivious ... (*She laughs*) No? Viciously Energetic And Lingering ...

They both laugh

Guy Vomitmaking Especially At Lunchtime ...

Fay screams with laughter

Fay (*recovering, glancing at her watch*) Your friend's late ...

Guy Yes. She is. I'm beginning to get a bit worried. I would have picked her up in the car only she's very independent and she does like to make her own way.

Fay Why not?

Guy Quite.

Fay Has she got far to come?

Guy No, only a bus ride. From Wellfield Flats.

Fay Oh, yes. I know. Near the park?

Guy That's it.

Fay Wellfield Flats. Aren't those for old people?

Guy That's right.

Fay Oh, I see. She works there, does she? As a nurse?

Guy No, no. She lives there.

Fay Lives there?

Guy Yes. Only—well, it's rather tricky. She's a proud old soul and she always hates it when people know she lives at Wellfield. So, if you could try not to mention it, I'd be grateful. You know what they're like at that age . . .

Fay What age?

Guy Well, she doesn't let on but my guess is early seventies . . .

Fay Seventies?

Guy But you'd never know it. She's up and down flights of stairs like nobody's business. She nursed my wife through a lot of her illness. I've always been grateful to her for . . .

He tails off. Fay is weeping with laughter

You all right?

Fay Yes, yes . . . (*Recovering a fraction*) And she's coming here? Tonight?

Guy Well, I hope so . . .

Fay I can't wait to see Ian's face . . .

Guy Ian?

Fay Dear God, this is wonderful . . . I love you. I love you.

Guy You needn't worry about the pictures. She's very broadminded. She's a game old bird, she really is. You'll like her.

Fay (*re-composing herself*) I'm sure. I'm sure.

Guy (*more dubious*) I hope Ian will get on with her but . . .

This starts Fay laughing again. She lies on the sofa and flails her legs

(*Confused*) Sorry, I'm not quite with all this I'm . . .

Fay sits up suddenly and listens

Fay Shh. He's back. Listen. Don't tell him about your friend. Keep her as a surprise.

Guy A surprise?

Fay Please . . .

Guy All right. Why?

Ian enters brandishing a Tequila bottle

Ian All over the bloody place. Driven five miles for this. Hi ya, Guy. Hallo, doll. You going to fix us one . . .?

Fay Sure. (*Taking the bottle*) Guy? Another one?

Guy Well, if it could be not quite so—

Fay Sure . . . (*she gathers up both their glasses*)

Ian Well, where's your friend, then?

Guy (*with a glance at Fay*) Oh, she's . . . she's . . . coming shortly.

Fay gives a stifled squeak of laughter

Ian What's the joke?

Fay Nothing. Nothing . . .

Ian There is someone else coming, I take it?

Fay (*going out*) Oh. Yes. Definitely someone else coming . . .

Fay goes out. Her laughter is heard ringing down the hall

Ian How many's she had, then?

Guy No idea.

Ian (*settling*) Like the pictures?

Guy Yes, I've been admiring them. Amazing.

Ian (*indicating one particular picture*) Fay can do that, you know.

Guy (*with disbelief*) Can she really? How incredible.

Ian One of the few women I know who can. You must get her to show you. (*Briskly*) Now, just before things start hotting up and getting out of hand—Could I just clear up this little business matter?

Guy Of course, of course.

Ian I won't beat about the bush. My partner and I have this little building firm as you probably know and we're contemplating buying a small piece of land which, as it happens, adjoins your factory.

Guy Yes, I know the piece. It so . . .

Ian Good. Well, there is a rumour—(*laughing*)—isn't there always?—that BLM may be intending to develop their existing premises. In which case, of course, the land in question could become a little more expensive. You follow?

Guy Yes. As a matter—

Ian All I'm asking is, is the rumour true?

Guy Well, all I can give you is the same answer I gave Dafydd. I honestly have no idea, but I'll try and find out. I've had no luck so far.

Ian (*slightly sharply*) Dafydd?

Guy Yes. I presume he's acting for you on this.

Ian Yes, yes. Maybe he is. (*Slight pause*) Don't take this the wrong way but—I could make this worth your while . . . I think I can speak for Fay and say we both could . . . (*He looks up at the picture and winks*) OK?

The doorbell rings

Ah, that'll be your friend. (*Yelling*) Doorbell, doll . . . (*To Guy*) The sort that likes to keep you waiting, is she? (*He grins*)

Guy Well, not if she can help it. She may have fallen over, of course . . .

Ian Fallen over? What is she? On skates?

Fay enters. She carries the drinks

Where is she then?

Fay You have to answer it.

Ian Why?

Fay Because you have to . . .

Ian Oh, all right. (*He moves to the door*)

Fay (*giving him a drink*) Here.

Ian (*taking it*) Ta.

Ian goes out

Fay (*calling after him*) You may need it. (*To Guy*) Quick, quick . . .

(*dragging him to the window*) Here. Have a look. Is that your friend? My God, it must be. (*She giggles*)

Guy Yes. That's Dilys. She looks a bit the worse for wear. Hope she's all right . . .

Fay Come on. Quick . . . (*She drags him again, this time to the door*) Bring your drink . . .

Guy Why, where . . .?

Fay Beddy-byes . . .

Guy Sorry?

Fay I'm in desperate need of veal. Now.

Guy (*as she drags him off*) Veal? What, in bed . . .

As they leave, Ian's voice is heard returning along the hall

Ian (*off*) Yes, well, perhaps you'd like to tidy up in the bathroom.

Ian enters speaking back to someone behind him

The light's just inside the door. Can you manage? That's it . . . Well done . . . (*He stands in the doorway with his drink. Stunned*) Bloody hellfire. (*He drains his glass*)

The lights fade on Ian and come up on a section of moonlit street

Guy, paralytically drunk, staggers into view. He stops under a street lamp

Guy (*bellowing into the night*) Fear not, good citizens, now abed. Matt of the Mint is here. The highwayman with the hole in the middle. Matt of the Mint V.E.A.L. Voraciously Enterprising Acrobatic Lover . . .

Guy starts to sing. Drunkenly unaccompanied at first and then, as the scene changes, as part of the rehearsal, along with Ted, Crispin and Jarvis. Mr Ames accompanying. Dafydd paces about watching

(*Singing, as Matt*) Let us take the road.
　　　　　　　　Hark! I hear the sound of coaches!
　　　　　　　　The hour of attack approaches,
　　　　　　　　To your arms, brave boys, and load,
　　　　　　　　See the ball I hold!
　　　　　　　　Let the chemists toil like asses,
　　　　　　　　Our fire their fire surpasses,
　　　　　　　　And our turns all our lead to gold.
　　　　　　　　Hoorah! Hoorah! Hoorah!

The song ends triumphantly. Ted, Crispin, Jarvis and Guy clink their papier mâché tankards with great dash. Bridget is back on the book

Dafydd Excellent. Bravo. Well done all, thank you. Couple of minutes and we're going on to Macheath and the ladies. Guy, please, could I have a moment?

Ted, Crispin and Jarvis start making their way backstage

No, no, Crispin, don't go away, boy. I need you in a minute.

Crispin remains

> *Ted and Jarvis exit*

(To Guy) He's like an animal, that boy. Only got to mention a coffee break and he's got his trousers round his knees. He's got both those girls on a string, you know. Linda and Bridget. It's not fair on the rest of us, is it ...? *(He laughs)*

Guy manages a smile

Now. Just a word, Guy. Fay's just had a chat with me. And. Well, it's Ian. According to Fay, he doesn't think he's going to be able to do the part after all. So. We are now without a Filch. Which is serious, because it's a very big part indeed. So. I think you know what's coming, Guy. What do you say? Filch. Could you do it?

The women, mustered by Bridget, are beginning to assemble on the other side of the stage. They are Rebecca, Fay, Hannah, Enid and Linda

Guy Well ...

Dafydd You know, a month ago I wouldn't even have considered asking you but—lately ... It's doing you good these dramatics. You're growing in confidence every day. Can I take it you'll agree?

Guy All right.

Dafydd Good man. *(He shakes Guy's hand)*

Guy And ... thank you.

Dafydd Don't thank me. Thank Fay. She suggested you straightaway. Of course, I agreed. *(Moving to address the assembly as a whole)* Ladies and gentlemen, I'd like to run the dance, please ... Take your places. But just before we do, unfortunately I have to announce yet another cast change. Unavoidably, Ian Hubbard has had to withdraw from his featured role as Filch and that part will now be taken by our all-purpose replacement, Mr Guy Jones.

All the women applaud

Rebecca I said he should have played it in the first place.

Dafydd There is, however, no truth in the rumour that, at his present rate of progress, he will shortly be taking over from yours truly. *(He laughs)*

One or two looks are exchanged

Thank you Mr Ames

A dance. The women parade around Crispin as Macheath

Women	Youth's the season made for joys,
Crispin	Love is then our duty,
Women	She alone who that employs,
Crispin	Well deserves her beauty.
Women	Let's be gay,
	While we may,
	Beauty's a flower, despised in decay.
	Youth's the season etc.

	Let us drink and sport to-day
Crispin	Ours is not tomorrow
Women	Love with youth flies swift away,
Crispin	Age is nought but sorrow
Women	Dance and sing,
	Time's on the wing,
	Life never knows the return of spring.
	Let us drink etc.

Dafydd (*calling encouragement*) Come on, Ladies, give it some body, some body . . . remember these are all pimps and whores. Horizontal women. All of them . . .

Rebecca (*softly but audibly*) Some of us may be . . .

Dafydd Come on, Linda, head up, try and sell it to us. Sell us your body, Linda . . .

Bridget (*with a laugh*) She couldn't give it away . . .

Dafydd Bridget, shut up . . . (*To the dancers*) That's it . . . good . . . better . . .

As the dance finishes

And we all look towards Macheath and curtsy . . .

The women are all turned in Guy's direction except for Enid who, quite correctly, is facing Crispin. Seeing she is the only one doing this she hastens to conform with the others

(*Seizing Enid and shaking her furiously*) No, not at him, at Macheath. Macheath . . . Oh, I give up . . .

The music ends

Crispin exits

All right. Thank you very much everyone. Fifteen minutes. Thank you.

Dafydd, Mr Ames and Bridget leave. The women follow, discussing as they go the events of the dance and in particular sympathizing, some of them anyway, with the luckless Enid

Bridget (*as they go*) The kettle's on . . .

Guy is left alone for a moment. He rises to follow the rest of them. He seems to us very pleased with life thus far

The Lights fade to a Black-out

CURTAIN

ACT II

The overall scene is very much the same; the time, a little later on into rehearsals. At the start, a light comes up on Crispin as Macheath

Crispin (*singing as Macheath*)

If the heart of a man is deprest with cares;
The mist is dispell'd when a woman appears;
Like the notes of a fiddle, she sweetly, sweetly
Raises the spirits and charms our ears.
Roses and lillies her cheeks disclose,
But her ripe lips are more sweet than those
Press her, caress her, with blisses her kisses
Dissolve us in pleasure, and soft repose.

As the song finishes, we crossfade to a café table. Basically a "four", at present it contains just Guy and Hannah. Used cups and plates and a cake stand with several cakes still remaining. Hannah is eating one of these. There is a tense air about the scene. Most of the tension, it would appear, being generated by Hannah

Hannah (*after a pause*) Well. What are you going to do about it? (*Pause*) I mean, you can't have both of us, can you? (*Pause*) You can't have your . . . (*She tails off as she looks at the cake stand*) You'll just have to make up your mind, Guy. Me or her.

Guy (*muttering unhappily*) It's not—that—easy . . .

Hannah What? What did you say?

Guy (*rather too loudly*) I said it's not that easy . . .

Hannah Sshh! Sshh! All right. Do you want the whole restaurant to hear us? (*Pause*) I mean, why do you want two of us, anyway?

Guy I don't want two of you—

Hannah Isn't one enough?

Guy I love you both in—different ways . . .

Hannah I'm glad to hear it. I suppose I'm the one who's good for sewing on buttons and doing your washing. That takes a great deal of arranging, I'll have you know. Using our machine while Dafydd's out of the way. Sorting out socks at midnight. (*A sudden practical thought*) You don't have any of his pants, do you? He's mislaid a pair.

Guy Sort of paisley patterned?

Hannah Those are them. If you have them, give me them back, will you?

Guy I think I've got them on, actually.

Hannah Oh, God. Guy.

Pause

Well, it's obvious you don't go to Fay for your washing. Despite all those pale clothes she wears, I always get the feeling that there's something very grubby underneath.

Guy Oh, come on, Hannah. (*Pause*) Have a cake.

Hannah I've had quite enough cake. And I'm sick to death of us meeting in cafés and pubs and bus shelters ...

Guy Well, where else can we go?

Hannah Nowhere. It's too small a town. Everybody knows.

Guy Yes, I know.

Hannah Except Dafydd, of course.

Guy No. I honestly don't think he does know. I thought at first he was turning a gigantic blind eye but ...

Hannah Dafydd doesn't know. He's amazing. Even the twins are suspicious. They've started calling that Daddy doll of theirs Guy. Fortunately, Dafydd just thinks they're starting early for bonfire night. (*Pause*) No, he doesn't want me—in that way—any more, so he assumes no one else could possibly—want me. (*Pause*) I'm not sure anyone does, really. (*She cries. Angry tears*)

Guy Hannah. Now, Hannah ...

Hannah (*savagely*) It's just damn lucky for you that Dafydd doesn't know about us, that's all I can say. Otherwise he'd sort you out, he really would. He'd beat you senseless. He'd punch you into a pulp. He'd smash your face in and jump on you and he'd kick you where it really hurt. And I'd laugh. Ha! Ha! He's bloody tough. He was a rugger player, you know ...

Guy Yes. Yes, he told me.

Hannah sobs

Please don't, Hannah. Please ... People are staring. I'll get the bill.

Hannah (*seeing someone behind Guy*) Oh, no ...

Guy What is it?

Hannah It's her. She followed us her. She's spying on us.

Guy Oh, Lord ...

Fay comes into view. She has evidently been shopping. She carries several bags

Fay Hallo, you two.

Hannah ignores her

Guy Hallo, Fay.

Fay What a funny place to come for tea. A right little clip joint ...

Hannah Is that why you're here?

Fay (*sitting at the table between them*) May I join you?

Hannah You most certainly may not.

Fay Thank you. Whew! I'm exhausted. You look terrible, Hannah. What is it, darling, hay fever?

Hannah I'm allergic, that's all. To certain smells.

Fay regards Hannah for a moment. A silence

Guy Look, this is all very awkward. I think it would be better if one of us left, I really do.
Fay It's all right. I'm not stopping . . .
Hannah Good.
Fay . . . I just wanted to give something to Guy.
Hannah What?

Fay produces a paper bag from amongst her shopping and passes it to Guy

Fay Here.
Hannah What is it?
Fay Private.
Hannah (*taking hold of the bag*) What?
Fay Mind your own business . . .
Hannah I demand to know what it is. I demand to know . . .
Fay Get your hands off . . .
Guy (*interceding; mildly*) Now, now. Now then. Come on, girls, people are . . . (*He smiles round the restaurant*)

Hannah and Fay stay deadlocked

Fay Then tell her to let go.
Hannah I refuse to allow her to walk in here and start giving you things . . .
Guy Hannah . . .
Hannah How dare she give you secret presents right under my nose. She's just trying to humiliate me. That's what she's doing.
Fay Let go.
Hannah No.
Guy Look. Let's be adult about this, shall we? (*Looking at them in turn*) Girls? Please. Look let me have it. And I'll open it. And then there'll be no secrets. All right? Hannah? Hannah . . .
Hannah All right. I want to see.
Guy Fay?
Fay (*shrugging*) Fine with me . . .

They release the bag to Guy

Guy Right. OK. Now then. (*He opens the bag and removes the contents*) Let's see what we have in . . . (*He holds a pair of paisley patterned pants*) Oh, God.
Fay They were under the bed. I didn't want you to catch cold. (*She giggles*)
Hannah (*looking at Fay with extreme loathing*) You total bitch. You total and utter grubby, smutty, grimy, unhygienic little bitch. (*Snatching at the pants*) Give me those. Give me those at once . . .
Guy (*holding them still*) Hannah . . .
Fay Don't do that . . .
Hannah Give them to me . . .
Fay (*joining in the tussle*) Let go, at once . . .
Guy Now this is silly. Now come on . . .

They tug

Hannah Give me these pants . . .
Fay Hannah, they are not yours. Now let go. They don't belong to you . . .
Hannah Oh, yes they do . . .
Fay Nonsense . . .
Guy I think they do actually, Fay.
Fay They're hers?
Hannah Yes.
Fay (*letting go*) Darling. I'm terribly sorry . . .
Guy (*also letting go*) I mean, when I say hers, I meant—
Fay Hannah, darling, who ever would have guessed. It just goes to show.
    Behind the most boring exterior . . .
Hannah (*stuffing the pants into her handbag*) How dare you do this? How
    dare you . . .?
Fay . . . lurks the weirdest of hang-ups . . .
Guy Fay, please . . .
Hannah (*rising and putting on her coat*) I'm not stopping here . . .
Fay Don't worry, darling, your secret is safe.
Hannah (*to Fay*) You'll be sorry for this. I promise you, you'll be sorry for
    this . . .

    Hannah goes out

Guy (*rising*) Oh, Fay . . . really. There was no need for that. Really . . .
Fay Oh. Are you going?
Guy Yes, of course. I've got to . . . (*he indicates Hannah*)
Fay Help her choose a jock strap . . .
Guy Fay, please, don't keep on. Those were Dafydd's . . .
Fay Dafydd's?
Guy Of course they were . . .
Fay Curiouser and curiouser . . .
Guy A mix-up in the wash. That's all . . .
Fay I shan't enquire further, darling. Don't worry. I'll see you this evening,
    then. At rehearsal.
Guy Rather.
Fay And I'll be in later, if you want to pop round . . .
Guy (*doubtfully*) Well . . . not this evening, Fay . . .
Fay By the way, Ian was asking if you'd heard anything yet. About the
    land.
Guy Oh. No. Sorry.
Fay Only Jarvis is not going to hang on for ever. If we don't buy it
    somebody else will.
Guy Jarvis? You mean it's Jarvis who owns it?
Fay (*feeling she may have said too much*) Yes. Didn't you know? I thought
    you did.
Guy No, I didn't realize he owned it.
Fay (*shrugging*) Not that it matters. The point is, have you been asking?
    Because that was part of our deal, darling, wasn't it?
Guy Deal? How do you mean?
Fay I mean, Ian did give up his role for you, didn't he? Filch.

Guy Oh, Filch. Yes. I didn't ask him to, you know.

Fay No, but you didn't say no, did you? But then you haven't actually said no to anything, have you? Not that I'm complaining. But I suppose Ian might. Eventually. If you don't come up with the goods.

Guy Well, I am ... I am asking round. Discreetly, of course.

Fay Oh, good. It'd be horrid if it all got nasty, wouldn't it? Bye-bye, darling.

Guy (*rather uneasily*) Bye ...

Guy exits rather unhappily

Fay sits on at her table for a minute, smiling to himself

A light comes up on Linda

Linda (*as Lucy, singing*)
>   Thus when a good huswife sees a rat
>   In her trap in the morning taken,
>   With pleasure her heart goes pit a pat,
>   In revenge for her loss of bacon.
>   Then she throws him
>   To the dog or cat,
>   To be worried, crushed and shaken.

As the song ends, Fay exits

General lights come up on Linda to reveal she is in rehearsal with both Hannah and Crispin, as Polly and Macheath. Also in attendance, Bridget with the prompt script, as usual. Dafydd is prowling the auditorium and, away in one corner paying little attention, Jarvis sits with a small portable cassette player clipped to his person and a pair of lightweight headphones clamped to his ears. He is in a private world of his own. Guy who has entered during the song also watches the ensuing rehearsal. Crispin stands holding a freestanding mock-up rehearsal gaol door, through which he plays the scene

Linda (*as Lucy*) Am I then bilk'd of my virtue? Can I have no reparation? Sure men were born to lye, and women to believe them! O Villain! Villain!

Hannah (*as Polly*) Am I not thy wife? Thy neglect of me, thy aversion to me, too severely proves it. Look on me. Tell me, am I not thy wife?

Linda (*as Lucy*) Perfidious wretch!

Hannah (*as Polly*) Barbarous husband!

Linda (*as Lucy*) Hadst thou been hang'd five months ago, I had been happy.

Hannah (*as Polly*) And I too. If you had been kind to me 'til Death, it would not have vex'd me. And that's no very unreasonable request, (though from a wife) to a man who hath not above seven or eight days to live.

Under this last exchange, Dafydd seeing Guy has joined the rehearsal, strolls over to him

Dafydd (*in a loud whisper*) Sorry. We're running a bit late. Be with you in a second.

Guy (*sotto*) OK.

Dafydd Bloody hard work it is with these three. This lad—great voice. But
he moves like something out of Austin Reed's window. And as for this
prissy little madam . . . (*he indicates Linda*) Look at her. I've seen rougher
trade on a health food counter . . .

The rehearsal continues

Linda (*as Lucy*) Are thou then married monster? . . . (*She hesitates*)
Bridget (*prompting loudly*) Art thou then married to another?
Linda (*as Lucy*) Art thou then married to another? Hast thou—
Bridget (*interrupting her*) Hast thou two wives, monster?
Linda All right, all right, I know it . . .
Bridget I was giving you the line . . .
Linda Yes, well, I knew it. I knew it, didn't I?

*Hannah wanders away from the exchange. There's evidently been quite a lot of
this sort of thing. Crispin remains amusedly detached. Dafydd returns his
attention to the rehearsal*

Dafydd All right, all right, girls. Come on, get on with it now.
Linda Every time I pause for breath, she reads out my line. Would you
kindly ask her not to, please?
Dafydd Bridget, don't read her lines out unless she asks for them. And
Linda, you stop pausing for so much breath.
Linda I have to breathe, don't I?
Bridget (*in an undertone*) Not necessarily . . .
Dafydd You can't take that long breathing onstage. You want to breathe
deeply, you breathe offstage in your own time . . . On we go. And Bridget,
shut up!
Bridget (*muttering to herself*) I thought the only reason I was here was to
prompt. I mean, what's the point of sitting here for three months . . .?
Dafydd Bridget. Shut up! Go on.

A slight pause. The women look at Crispin

Crispin Oh, it's my go, is it? Right. (*As Macheath*) If women's tongues can
cease for an answer—hear me.

Dafydd whimpers audibly at Crispin's effort

(*Looking out in Dafydd's direction*) I heard that . . .
Linda (*as Lucy*) I won't. Flesh and blood can't bear my usage.
Hannah (*as Polly*) Shall I not claim my own? Justice bids me speak. Sure,
my dear, there ought to be some preference shown to a wife! At least she
may claim the appearance of it. (*Pointedly in Guy's direction*) He must be
distracted with his misfortunes, or he could not use me thus!

Another silence. Hannah looks at Linda

Linda (*realizing belatedly that it's her*) Um. Oh. Yes. Um. Oh. Eee. (*She
twists herself in knots trying to remember; to Bridget, reluctantly*) What is
it, then?
Bridget (*prompting*) Oh . . .

Linda (*repeating her*) Oh . . .
Bridget (*forming the first syllable of "villain"*) V . . . v . . .
Linda (*with her*) V . . . v . . . vain . . . vish . . . voo . . . ver . . . ver . . .
Dafydd (*screaming from the back of the auditorium*) Look, what the hell is this, twenty bloody questions?
Linda (*wailing*) She won't tell me my line . . .
Dafydd Bridget, for God's sake, tell her her line . . .
Bridget You just told me not to. (*Reading rapidly*) Oh villain villain thou hast deceiv'd me I could even inform against thee with pleasure not a prude wishes more heartily to have facts against her intimate acquaintance . . .

Linda starts wailing during this monotone rendition by Bridget

Dafydd Bridget! That'll do . . .

Bridget stops

Bridget (*innocently*) What?
Hannah (*comforting Linda*) Now, come on, dear . . .
Linda (*scarcely audible, weeping*) She does that all the time. She keeps doing it. All the time . . .

Dafydd gives a vast groan of impatience

Hannah Just a minute, Dafydd, just a minute . . .

A very private women's huddle between Linda and Hannah that none of us can hear. Crispin, the root cause of all this, stands looking quite pleased with himself. He pulls faces at Dafydd through the jail door

Dafydd (*to Guy*) Look at that smirking oaf. I wish to God they were professionals. Then I could sack them. These bastards, they've got you over a barrel. Unless you say well done all the time they don't turn up. What are those two doing? It's like a loose scrum. (*Yelling*) Come on, injury time's over. Give her a slice of lemon, change her shorts, and get her back on the field.
Hannah (*leaving Linda, to Dafydd*) Right. She's all right. (*To Linda*) All right?

Linda nods and resumes her position

Linda (*as Lucy, in a colourless tone, growing increasingly inaudible*) O villain, villain! (*She sniffs*) Thou has deceiv'd me. (*Sniff*) I could even inform against thee with pleasure. Not a prude wishes more heartily to have facts against her intimate acquaintance, than I now wish to have facts against thee. I would have her satisfaction, and they should all out . . . (*She peters out*)

During Linda's speech Dafydd has moved closer and closer to her in an attempt to hear

Dafydd And . . . Mr Ames! Don't tell me he's died now. Mr Ames . . .
Mr Ames (*cheerily*) Hallo?
Dafydd Song.

Mr Ames Sorry. (*He starts to play*)

Hannah (*singing, as Polly*)	I'm bubbled.
Linda (*singing, as Lucy*)	I'm bubbled.
Hannah	Oh how I am troubled!
Linda	Bambouzled and bit!
Hannah	My distresses are doubled.
Linda	When you come to the tree, should the hangman refuse,
	These fingers, with pleasure, could fasten the noose.
Hannah	I'm bubbled, etc.

The song ends. The scene resumes without pause

(*Speaking, as Polly*) And hast thou the heart to persist in disowning me?

Crispin (*as Macheath*) And hast thou the heart to persist in persuading me that I am married? Why, Polly, dost thou seek to aggravate my misfortunes?

Dafydd groans again at this rendition

Linda (*as Lucy*) Really, Miss Peachum, you but expose yourself.

Bridget sniggers

Besides ... (*Crossing to Bridget; furiously*) Will you stop laughing at me? Will you stop laughing?

Dafydd (*from the back of the auditorium*) Hey, hey, hey, hey ...

Bridget It was funny ...

Hannah Linda ...

Linda I'll soon make you stop laughing.

Linda grabs the unprepared Bridget by her hair and hauls her off her chair and onto the floor

Bridget (*furiously*) OW ...!

Crispin (*with great relish*) Wey-hey!

Linda I'll teach you, I'll teach you ...

Bridget Now, let go. Let go, I'm warning you ...

Hannah Oh, dear heavens. That's it. That's it. No more ...

Dafydd (*ineffectually, trying to part them*) Now come on, girls, come on ...

Jarvis's attention has been attracted by the scrap onstage

Jarvis (*to Dafydd, loudly because of his headphones*) Good scrap that. Very convincing. First class.

Dafydd Oh, shut up.

Jarvis does not hear but smiles. The girls are fighting in earnest now. Close combat stuff, on the floor, rolling over and over, both seeking for an advantage. Bridget's greater strength is matched by Linda's white hot fury. Mr Ames, at Crispin's beckoning, starts up another song. During the course of this, the fight continues silently until Guy and Dafydd manage to prise the girls apart. All this in mimed silence, although presumably in reality the din is quite loud

Crispin, with unusual relish, sings with Mr Ames

Crispin ⎱
Mr Ames ⎰ *(together)*   How happy could I be with either,
                              Were t'other dear charmer away!
                              But while you thus teaze me together,
                              To neither a word will I say;
                              But tol de rol, etc.

As the song finishes, "normal sound" is resumed. The combatants are panting and exhausted. So are the rescuers. Guy is holding Bridget, Hannah holds Linda. Dafydd stands between them, gasping to regain his breath, before speaking. Jarvis has watched it all from his ringside seat with great enjoyment

Dafydd *(at length)* All right now . . . listen to me . . . both of you . . .

Bridget attempts to struggle free from Guy. Guy clings on

   Now come along, Bridget. Bridget! Bridget . . .

Dafydd makes to slap Bridget's face. She quietens. He goes to pat her instead. She snaps at his hand and he all but loses his fingers

   Jesus! All right . . .

Linda starts to struggle, too

Hannah I can't hold her much . . .
Dafydd *(to Hannah)* All right, take her backstage. Backstage. Run her under a tap.

Hannah starts to drag Linda off

   (To Guy) And her. Outside. *(Assisting Guy with Bridget)* All right, I've got her. Come on. Outside, you. Outside.

   Hannah takes Linda off. Guy and Dafydd take Bridget out lifting her between them. Dafydd returns almost immediately

Guy presumably remains outside in case Bridget decides to return

Dafydd now turns his attention to the smirking Crispin

   As for you, you sniggering Herbert. This is all your fault. You were entirely to blame for that.
Crispin Bollocks. *(He goes to leave)*
Dafydd *(going after him)* I've a good mind to sort you out, boy, I really have.
Crispin *(turning suddenly, violently)* Right you are. You're on.
Dafydd *(taken aback somewhat by this change of tone)* What?
Crispin Come on, then . . .
Dafydd No, that's not the way. Violence is no solution.
Crispin I've been longing to have a go at you. Come on.

Crispin starts to advance slightly on Dafydd. He, in turn, retreats rather apprehensively

You've been getting up my nose for a few weeks now . . .

Crispin advances on Dafydd, making the latter retreat, during Dafydd's next speech

Dafydd Now come on, boy, be your age. Ah ah. Now, now. I'm a . . . I'm a middle-aged man, you know. Very nearly. That wouldn't be fair. Let's be reasonable. . . . Now, don't you . . . don't you try it . . . I'm a lawyer, you know . . . I could have you for . . . I won't, of course, if you don't . . .

Dafydd is now nose to nose with Crispin unable to retreat further

(*Nervously*) Well, now what? Eh? (*He laughs*)
Crispin Well . . .
Dafydd Yes?
Crispin How about this for starters?

Crispin brings his knee up sharply and moves back. Dafydd gives a fearful whistling sound and bends double

   Hannah and Guy both return separately to witness this

Hannah Dafydd . . .
Guy Hoy . . .
Crispin (*cheerfully*) 'Bye all . . .

   Crispin strolls out

Dafydd (*in pain*) OOoooorrrggg.
Jarvis (*who was watching this*) No, that wasn't as convincing as the other one . . .
Dafydd (*glaring at Jarvis, his face twisted in malignant pain*) I'll kill him. I'll kill that old bastard . . .
Jarvis (*smiling, unhearing*) You don't mind an opinion, do you?
Guy You OK?
Hannah Is he all right?
Guy Yes, I think he's been hit in the . . .
Hannah (*sympathetically*) Oh, yes. It's very painful there, isn't it?
Dafydd Of course it's bloody painful . . .
Guy Cold water helps . . . I think.
Hannah Right. Well, you . . . (*She starts to lead Dafydd away*) You'd better come and sit with Linda. You can have the sink after her . . .

They start going off, Hannah picking up Linda's bag on their way. Dafydd groans

   Carefully, dear. That's it . . .

   Hannah and Dafydd exit

Guy (*to himself*) Oh, well . . .
Jarvis (*removing his headphones and offering them to Guy*) Have a listen to that. Tell me what you think it is.

Guy somewhat reluctantly puts on the headphones. Whatever he hears is very loud and not too pleasant. He hastily takes off

Guy God. What is it?

Jarvis Give up? That is an actual recording of an 1812 Boulton and Watt beam engine which is still used to this day for pumping water to the summit of the Kennet and Avon canal.

Guy Good heavens.

Jarvis It lifts one ton of water forty feet on each stroke of the engine.

Guy Amazing.

Jarvis That's what I've been listening to for the past hour.

Guy A beam engine?

Jarvis Aye.

Guy What, all evening?

Jarvis No, no, no. This is called *Vanishing Sounds in Britain*. Issued by the BBC. All vanishing sounds . . .

Guy Well, listening to that, it's probably a good job, isn't it? (*He laughs*)

Jarvis (*not hearing*) What's that? (*He switches off the recorder*) No, I gave the record to the wife last Christmas but she wasn't so keen . . .

Guy Look. May I have a quick word with you? (*Looking round to see that they're alone*) It's about a piece of land that apparently belongs to you. Round the back of the BLM factory. Do you know it?

Jarvis I not only know it. I own it.

Guy Yes.

Jarvis I'll tell you a very interesting little tale about that bit of land . . .

Guy (*his heart sinking*) Oh, really . . .

Jarvis That land was purchased by my grandfather, old Joshua Pike, for the benefit of his employees. He were a philanthropist and a deeply religious man—chapel, you see—but his other passion, apart from 't firm, were cricket. Cricket mad. You with me?

Guy Aye. Yes.

Jarvis Well, he bought that land off a widow woman and he had his lads, his workers, levelling and draining and returfing it—in their own time, mind—not his. And, well, when it were finished—well, some said it were the finest strip for a hundred mile or more. Like a billiard pool. And he said to the lads, there you are, lads, go to it. That's my gift to you. That's my bounty.

Guy Wonderful.

Jarvis Only one thing—bearing in mind he were a chapel man—not on Sundays, lads. Never on the sabbath. Well, any road up, year or so later, he's out for a stroll one Sunday afternoon with his children and his grandchildren—taking the air, like—and what should he spy as he's passing the cricket field but a bunch of workers laughing and joking and chucking a ball about like it were Saturday dinner time. And the old man says nowt. Not at the time. But the next day, Monday morning first thing, he sends in his bulldozers and diggers and ploughs and he digs that land up from one end to the other. Then he sets fire to 't pavilion and he puts up a twelve foot wooden fence. Palings. And to this day, not a ball has been thrown on that field. That's the sort of man he was. Me grandfather. Dying breed.

Guy Another Vanishing Sound of Britain. Yes . . . (*After what he hopes is a*

respectful pause) The point is, with regard to this land . . . There is a
rumour, unconfirmed I may add, that BLM are contemplating buying it.
Possibly. In which case it could be worth a bit. If you were considering
selling it.

Jarvis considers this

So.

Jarvis Say no more.

Guy You follow me.

Jarvis I'm glad of the information. I trust you. You're a Scotty. And I'll see
you're looked after, don't worry.

Guy No, I don't need looking after. Really.

Jarvis Then why are you telling me?

Guy Well, I—thought you ought to know—it's just that I wouldn't want
people to put one over on you. Friendly.

Jarvis (*laughing sceptically*) Friendly? Oh, aye? That's a good one.

Guy Well, if you don't believe me . . .

Jarvis Don't come the friendly with me, friend. I've a few years to go yet but
when I leave this earth, I'll be leaving it fair and square. Same as me father
did and me grandfather. I owe nothing to no one. They're all paid off. I've
paid off my business. I've paid off my family. There's no claim on me from
any quarter. And I don't intend to start making exceptions with you. You
see me right. I'll see you right. Right?

Guy Right.

*Rebecca comes in from the street. She is in time to catch the end of this
conversation. She looks at them a trifle suspiciously*

Rebecca Hello.

Jarvis Aye.

Guy Good evening.

Rebecca Has Dafydd got to us yet?

Guy No. I don't think he's got to very much, actually . . .

Rebecca How unsurprising. Where is he? Back there?

Guy Yes.

Rebecca I'll sort them out then. I've had enough of this . . .

Rebecca goes backstage

Jarvis I've paid her off and all. My mother's ninety-two. She's paid off.

Guy You paid your mother off?

Jarvis A hundred quid a week, tax-free and a bungalow in Paignton. She's
not complaining. (*As he moves to go backstage*) You'll be paid off. Don't
worry . . .

Jarvis exits

*Guy, alone and as keen as ever, decides to have a quick private rehearsal. He
takes up his script. He reads other people's lines but tries to speak his own
without looking*

Guy (*reading*) "Come hither Filch" . . . blurr, blurrr, blurr . . . (*He skips*)

Where was your post last night, my boy? (*Without the script*) I ply'd at the opera, Madam; and considering 'twas neither dark nor rainy, so that there was no great hurry in getting chairs and coaches, made a tolerable on't. These seven handkerchiefs, Madam. (*He checks the script and is pleased to see he got it right*)

Guy is about to continue when Dafydd appears. He is very subdued and is sipping a beaker of tea

How are you feeling?

Dafydd Oh, pretty good. Like a man who's just spent his wedding night with an electrified steam shovel . . .

Guy nods sympathetically

Well. Now we are in a hole. If that boy doesn't come back we're over the dead ball line, I can tell you. Trying to do *The Beggar's Opera* without a Macheath is a bit of a non-starter even for Peter Brook. So. (*Pause*) Oh, it makes you want to . . . Who cares, anyway? Who cares?

Guy I do.

Dafydd Ah, Guy, Guy. My rock. But nobody really cares. Not in this country. Anything you want to mention's more important than theatre to most of them. Washing their hair, cleaning their cars . . . If this was Bulgaria or somewhere we'd have peasants hammering on the doors. Demanding satisfaction or their money back. This place, you tell them you're interested in the arts, you get messages of sympathy. Get well soon. Well, maybe they're right. Why beat your brains out? Every time I vow I'm just going to have a ball. I'm not going to take any of it seriously. It's just a play, for God's sake . . . And every time it gets like this. Desperate. Life and death stuff. Look at me. You'd think to look at me I was in really serious trouble. While all that's happened, in fact, is that a play might not happen. That's all. But of course the irony is that outside these four walls, in the real world out there, I actually am in serious trouble and I couldn't give a stuff. Now that really does raise questions, doesn't it? If I were my psychiatrist I'd be worried that all was not well. And I'd be right.

Guy (*cautiously*) Any— particular sort of trouble?

Dafydd (*evasively*) Well, apart from being beaten up by a singing Yahoo . . . nothing very original. I don't know. Things, you know. Hannah. Things like that. (*Pause*) She's a bloody deep-freeze of a woman. That's the trouble. Physically. I mean, she's great in other ways. Wonderful at keeping the home going and things. I mean without her . . . (*He smiles*) I call her my Swiss Army Wife, you know. No man should be without one. (*He laughs*) Yes, yes . . . It's just that she's—she's got a blade missing, if you know what I mean. Always has had. Isn't her fault, of course. Just not in her nature. Right from our wedding night. Ice tongs to lift her nightdress, I'm telling you . . .

Guy You didn't . . . find out—before you were married?

Dafydd Well, not from my part of Wales, boy. Not too hot on sale or return there, you know. Mind you, I assumed she'd thaw. Given a little warmth. And, you know, general encouragement. (*With more passion, suddenly*)

God, it's not that I didn't try . . . I really wanted to make it work, I really did. The nights I spent—battering at those damn defences of hers. But nothing. Knock one down she'd build another.

Guy (*trying to lighten it*) Well. You managed to have twins . . .

Dafydd (*darkly*) Yes. Well, we never talk about that. Never.

Guy Ah . . .

Dafydd Sorry, Guy. Bloody bore. I'm sorry. Why should I bore you with me and Hannah? Sorry . . . Don't know what came over me. I think it takes a kick in the crutch to make a man painfully aware of his own mortality . . .

Rebecca returns

(*Irritably*) Yes?

Rebecca Sorry to interrupt. First, I thought you'd like to know that the tannoy's on . . .

Dafydd Oh, God . . .

Rebecca And second, in a vain attempt to prevent Hannah from hearing, we had a meeting . . .

Dafydd Oh, yes. And?

Rebecca Well, what are we going to do? Scrap the production? I mean that boy, from all accounts, doesn't intend to come back, does he? So what do we do?

Dafydd I don't know what we do. You tell me. You're the one who keeps holding bloody meetings. Next time try inviting me. Maybe I can make a few suggestions.

Rebecca Very well, to start with. We need a new Macheath. Agreed?

Dafydd Yes. And where are we going to find him? Eh?

Rebecca Well . . . (*She looks towards Guy*)

Guy Ah.

Dafydd You mean Guy?

Rebecca He's the natural choice, isn't he? It's either him or Ian Hubbard . . .

Dafydd Oh God, anyone rather than Ian Hubbard . . .

Rebecca (*pointing towards the tannoy mic*) Shh!

Dafydd Sorry. (*In a whisper*) Could you do it?

Guy I—

Rebecca Do it? He'd love it . . .

The lights close down to a single spot on Guy

Rebecca and Dafydd leave

Guy (*singing, as Macheath*)
> Which way shall I turn me—How can I decide!
> Wives, the day of our death, are as fond as a bride.
> One wife is too much for most husbands to hear,
> But two at a time there's no mortal can bear.
> This way, and that way, and which way I will,
> What would comfort the one, t'other wife would take ill.

At the end of the song, the lights come up on Rebecca's garden. A seat. A garden table

Guy stands looking round

Rebecca (*hailing him*) Yoo-hoo! Over here, Guy. It's so sweet of you to pop round. Excuse the midges, won't you? Would you like a cup of tea? Shall I ring for some tea?

Guy No. No, thank you. Had my tea at home, just now.

Rebecca Sure? A sherry or something?

Guy No. Thanks all the same. Not with rehearsals in a minute.

Rebecca (*picking up her own glass*) Quite right, quite right. You put the rest of us to shame, Guy. Mind you, I don't think it would matter that much if I drank myself silly. They always manage to hide me behind a piece of scenery anyway ... (*She laughs*)

Guy laughs politely

Do sit down. (*Proffering a cigarette box*) Do you? No. You are good. None of the vices. Practically (*She smiles*) We all think you're going to be an absolutely wonderful Macheath.

Guy Thank you.

Rebecca I take the view that Dafydd's terribly lucky to get you. Whatever the price.

Guy I'm sorry?

Rebecca There's no need to be sorry. You've jollied us up no end, Guy. All of us. In our different ways.

Guy Well ...

Rebecca Now, what I'm really hoping is that you're going to make my day as well. After all, you've made nearly everybody else's. One way or another. It must be my turn, mustn't it? Surely?

Rebecca smiles at him warmly. Guy shifts a little uncomfortably. They are left thus as a light comes up on Ted, Enid and Jarvis

Ted ⎫
Enid ⎬ (*together, singing*)
Jarvis ⎭

In the days of my youth I could bill like a dove,
Fa, la, la, etc.
Like a sparrow at all times was ready for love,
Fa, la, la, etc.
The life of all mortals in kissing should pass,
Lip to lip while we're young—then the lip to the glass,
Fa, la, la etc.

At the end of the song the lights return to their previous state. Rebecca and Guy have been chattering away

Rebecca Now. This little favour I wanted to ask ... (*Seeing Guy's expression*) Don't look so terrified. It's not what you're thinking ...

Guy No, no. I was—

Rebecca God forbid. Six years sharing a mattress with Jarvis cured me of that. No, it's just that I understand you and he were talking the other evening ...

Guy Yes? Oh, yes. About the—

Rebecca About out little bit of land.

Guy Yes. As a matter of fact I wanted to talk about that too, actually . . .

Rebecca Good.

Guy (*fumbling in his pocket*) The point is I've—well, it's rather awkward—(*He produces a bulging envelope*) I got this in the post this morning.

Rebecca Oh, how gorgeous. (*Peering*) What is it? I'm sorry, I haven't my glasses.

Guy It's five hundred pounds.

Rebecca Oh, super.

Guy In notes. Cash.

Rebecca Lucky you. What happened? Someone passed away?

Guy Not—so far as I know. No. I rather thought it came from you.

Rebecca Me?

Guy Well, rather from Jarvis.

Rebecca Jarvis?

Guy I think so.

Rebecca It sounds very unlikely. You'd be the first person who managed to get money out of Jarvis. None of his wives ever could, I can tell you . . . Two of them died trying, poor things.

Guy I'm pretty certain it is from him.

Rebecca What does it say? With love from Jarvis?

Guy Of course not. It's—

Rebecca Then how do you know? Why on earth would my husband send you five hundred pounds?

Guy Because I—I warned him about this rumour. About the land. I can't at present find any foundation in truth in it, but there's this rumour that—

Rebecca (*slightly impatiently*) Yes, I've heard the rumour.

Guy You have?

Rebecca Oh, yes.

Guy Well. I told Jarvis simply because I was anxious that he shouldn't be taken advantage of. Or you.

Rebecca Well, that's awfully sweet of you. Thank you. Of course, it could work both ways, couldn't it? I mean, supposing this rumour wasn't true but everyone assumed it was, then the price would go up and Jarvis would be laughing. And the joke would be on these very unscrupulous people that you've so kindly been warning us about. Which would be a sort of poetic justice, wouldn't it?

Guy Ah.

Rebecca Of course, the whole thing would be helped tremendously if someone strategically placed like yourself did nothing to deny the rumour. Even, dare one say it, encouraged it?

Guy Oh, I don't think I could . . .

Rebecca No, no, heaven forbid. That's entirely up to your conscience. Anyway, you've got much too much on your mind already with Macheath. We mustn't worry you. Just remember, though, when they're all clapping and cheering you on the first night, it was me who got you the part. Remember that . . .

Guy Yes. And I'm very grateful. I—

Rebecca (*with the barest glance at her watch*) Now, we must dash, mustn't we? We don't want to keep them waiting. Do you have your car? (*She is moving away as she speaks*)

Guy Yes, thank you . . . You know, I'd really love to know how this rumour started. It's extraordinary . . .

Rebecca looks at Guy for a second and then realizes his question was without guile

Rebecca Well, I suspect that's something we shall never know, shall we? Any of us. Coming?

Guy (*indicating the envelope on the table*) What about—? What shall I do with this? The money?

Rebecca That's up to you, surely. Have fun with it, I should.

Guy I can't accept it. Possibly.

Rebecca Don't be so absurd.

Guy No. If I took it, that would be . . . it'd be . . .

Rebecca Well, suit yourself what you do with it. Only for heaven's sake don't leave it there. Or people might get the idea you were giving it to us. And that wouldn't look good at all, would it?

Rebecca exits

Guy stares at the envelope undecided. He half moves away. He stops. After a second or so he returns to the money. He takes it up and pockets it. As he does so the lights change and we are back in the rehearsal room. Guy now changes into his basic Macheath costume. He is assisted in this by several of the women in the company who fuss round him. Amongst these are Hannah, Fay, Enid and Linda. All of these are in part, most, or all, of their costume. The production is entering its final phase. From hereon we are very conscious that the production is "lit". While this activity ensues silently, Bridget, also in costume for her role as Jenny Diver, sings

Bridget   Before the barn-door crowing,
                                  The cock by hens attended,
                                  His eyes around him throwing,
                                  Stands for a while suspended,
                                  Then one he singles from the crew,
                                  And cheers the happy hen;
                                  With how do you do, and how do you do,
                                  And how do you do again.

The other women sing with Bridget at the chorus

As the song finishes, the lighting rehearsal continues. Guy remains midstage

The women and Mr Ames leave the stage

The rehearsal has apparently been delayed for technical reasons

Dafydd enters from the lighting box carrying a vast lighting plan

Dafydd Sorry, Guy. We'll be underway pretty soon now. If nothing else blows up on us. (*Indicating the lighting box; confidentially*) He's slow this electrician, though. Twenty minutes changing a colour. Unbelievable. I mean, why volunteer to light a show if you suffer from vertigo? He knew there'd be ladders. Man's a half-wit, he should ...

Another single light comes up on stage

(*Calling to the box*) Thank you, Raymond, that's—that's lovely. (*Standing in a vivid orange patch of light, to Guy*) This look like firelight to you?
Guy (*uncertainly*) No. Not a lot.
Dafydd No, nor me. I'll cut it later. Better leave it for now. It took him three hours to focus ... (*Calling again*) Yes, we're wild about that, Raymond. We like it very much. (*Consulting his plan*) Could I see your number eighteen now, please? That's my number fifteen your number eighteen. Thank you. (*To Guy*) Haven't even got the same bloody numbers, these plans.

A light comes up

No, that's number seventeen, Raymond. That's your number seventeen. My number twelve. The one I want to see is my number fifteen your number eighteen.
Raymond (*a distant voice*) That is number eighteen ...
Dafydd What's that? No, that's number seventeen. My number twelve. I don't want number seventeen. I want number eighteen. My number eighteen your number fifteen.
Raymond I haven't got a number fifteen ...
Dafydd No, hang on, as you were. *My* number fifteen. *Your* number eighteen.

Another lamp comes on

No, no, that's number fifty-six. That shouldn't even be bloody plugged up ... Hang on, hang on. For God's sake. I'm coming up, Raymond. And somebody, please open some doors. It's sub-tropical in here ...

Dafydd goes up to the lighting box

Guy, on his own, walks about the stage getting the feel of his costume and feeling slightly sick with nerves. He clears his throat and swings his arms

Hannah enters with the jacket of his costume

Hannah (*handing it to Guy*) Here. That should be better.
Guy Thank you.

Guy puts on the jacket. There is an awkward formality between them

Hannah Let me know if it's still uncomfortable ...
Guy No, no. This is perfect.

Dafydd emerges briefly in the doorway of the lighting box

Dafydd Try circuit twelve plugged into twenty-two. Twenty-two, Raymond. Twenty-two. My ... what the hell is it, it's my auxiliary ninety-six. Look, Raymond, next time you re-number the bloody patch field you might tell everybody else about it, will you ...?

Dafydd goes inside again

Hannah Guy . . .?
Guy Yes?
Hannah Why haven't you phoned?
Guy Oh, Hannah . . .
Hannah (*moving to him*) What is it? What have I done?

They stand together, instinctively clear of the lights and thus out of Dafydd's view

Guy Look, I've been . . . I've had all this on my mind, haven't I? The play . . .
Hannah Is that more important than us?
Guy No, it's . . . We've been together every evening, for God's sake.
Hannah If you call that being together . . .
Guy Well, it's been very difficult, Hannah. I've only had just over a week to learn the thing . . .

A brilliant light strikes them both as Raymond locates another circuit. Instinctively, they both move away

   Dafydd emerges from the box again

Dafydd That's fine. Keep that one, don't lose it. Now twenty-seven and twenty-eight should be paired. . . . Let's have a look at those. (*Muttering*) Within the next twenty-five minutes if possible . . .

   Dafydd goes into the box again

Guy Look, there's no point in discussing this now. We can't decide anything in the middle of a—
Hannah (*loudly*) Well, when can we?

Two more lights illuminate them suddenly

   Dafydd emerges again

Hannah and Guy look up at Dafydd

Dafydd Sorry, my loves, I'll be with you in a minute. Try not to get impatient . . .

   Dafydd goes again

Hannah and Guy move out of the lights again

Guy All right. If you want to talk about it, we will . . . OK. I think it's all got to stop. All right? I think it's been tremendous fun and I think you're wonderful, but it simply has to stop.
Hannah (*stunned*) What are you talking about? Stop?

   Dafydd appears again

Dafydd Perches one and two. Again, they should be paired . . .

   Dafydd goes

Hannah Why? Why?
Guy Well. For one thing, Dafydd ...
Hannah Dafydd?
Guy Yes.
Hannah Who the hell cares about Dafydd?

More lights come up on them again

Dafydd appears again

Dafydd I don't like the look of those two.

Hannah and Guy move again

Lose them. Give me the other side. Perches seven and eight, I think.

Dafydd goes

Hannah What's Dafydd got to do with anything?
Guy Hannah, Dafydd has everything to do with everything. He is your
husband and he's my friend. And if I felt that I was responsible for your
leaving him ...
Hannah I'm leaving him anyway, whether you stay or not, so that has
nothing to do with it ...

*A light, this time illuminating them brilliantly from the knees downwards
comes up. Guy and Hannah both jump instinctively*

Guy (*irritably*) Get away ...

Dafydd appears

Dafydd Well, those are no earthly use at all, Raymond. They're lighting his
socks. He'd have to be a midget. What do you think we're doing, Snow
White? FOH four then. Let's try that ...

Dafydd goes

Hannah No, I know exactly what you're doing. You're using Dafydd as an
excuse to ditch me, that's all ...
Guy That just isn't true ...

More lights come on, replacing the others. Guy and Hannah are clear of them

Hannah Don't try and pretend to me that you'd consider Dafydd for one
single moment ...
Dafydd (*calling*) I say, you two ...
Hannah ... if it didn't suit you. It didn't worry you two weeks ago ...
Dafydd (*calling*) I say, you two—
Guy I think he wants us ...
Hannah (*angrily*) Yes?

Dafydd comes onstage

Dafydd Sorry. Were you running lines? Look, just to save time, would you
mind standing for me? I just want to check this focus.

He moves Guy and Hannah into the lights

Just move into that one, that's right ... Bit further forward, Hannah. Thank you. Just hold it there.

Dafydd moves away into the auditorium to check the effect

Hannah (*as he goes, muttering*) Feeblest excuse I have ever heard in my life ...

Dafydd Hannah, dear, be Annie Anderson for a minute, would you? She's a little taller than you—can you just go up on your toes?

Hannah goes up on tip-toe

Bit more. Thank you.

Hannah (*awkwardly*) I would have preferred it if you'd been honest and said another woman ...

Dafydd Guy, my love ...

Hannah Which, of course, it is.

Dafydd Guy, could you go down to Tony Moffit's size? Would you mind ...?

Guy crouches low

Guy About here?

Dafydd Fine. Just hold it. (*He considers for a second*) No, that's not going to work, Raymond. Show me something else ...

During the next, a number of lamps flash on and off the contorted pair, as Raymond offers Dafydd, who is pacing the auditorium, alternative light sources. Dafydd rejects each in turn

Hannah (*on the verge of tears again, softly*) I was prepared to give up everything for you, you know ...

A lamp comes on

Guy (*softly*) I know, I know ...

Dafydd (*calling*) No.

Hannah (*softly*) My home, my marriage, even my children ...

The light goes off and another comes on

Guy (*softly*) I don't think you were, Hannah, not if it came to it ...

Dafydd (*calling*) No ...

Hannah (*softly*) I meant every single thing I said to you ...

The light goes off and another goes on

Guy (*softly*) I meant everything I said, too ...

Dafydd (*calling*) No. Not in a million years ...

Hannah (*softly*) You were playing around with Fay and—God knows who else. You used me, Guy ...

The light goes off and another goes on

Guy (*louder*) That is a lie—

Dafydd (*calling*) Yes! That's it ... What number's that?

Dafydd rejoins them onstage to check his plan. Hannah lets out an involuntary moan of misery

    (*Looking up at them*) Oh sorry, relax, loves. Sorry. Thanks for your help. (*He resumes his task*)

A sob from Hannah as they relax their positions

    Mr Ames returns, now in all but full costume

Guy Hannah ...

Dafydd What's the matter with her?

Guy Er ...

Dafydd (*peering at her*) You daft halfpenny, you been staring into lights again, haven't you? How many times do I have to tell you? Shut your eyes, girl ... (*He cuffs her affectionately*)

Dafydd moves away towards the lighting box

Guy (*imploring*) Hannah ...

Hannah (*deeply miserable*) Oh, Guy ...

Dafydd Now, let me see with that added to it, the state of cue fifty-four C ...

    Dafydd goes back into the lighting box

Hannah I do love you so much, Guy ...

Guy I love you, Hannah ...

Music starts under. As it does a rather romantic light setting comes up. Presumably Cue fifty-four C

Hannah (*singing, as Polly*)

                O what pain it is to part!
                Can I leave thee, can I leave thee?
                O what pain it is to part!
                Can thy Polly ever leave thee?
                But lest death my love should thwart,
                And bring thee to the fatal cart,
                Thus I tear thee from my bleeding heart!
                Fly hence, and let me leave thee.

Guy
Hannah } (*together*)   But lest death my love should thwart etc.

    As the song is ending, Hannah runs from the stage

Guy is left standing miserably. The last notes cut off as the lights resume a more neutral state

    Dafydd emerges from the box

Dafydd (*calling back behind him*) Save that now, Raymond. Save it and replug for the top of the show. God, I think we're there ... (*He comes down on to the stage*) Sorry Guy. You've been wonderfully patient. Thank you.

Guy Dafydd . . .
Dafydd Yes, my love . . .
Guy I feel I do have to talk to you about something . . .
Dafydd Oh, yes? (*Calling*) Give me the workers, would you, Raymond?
And will someone on stage management bring me the A ladders . . .? Yes.
Sorry, Guy. What's the problem?
Guy Well—it's a ridiculous time to say it but . . .

The lights switch to working lights

Dafydd (*yelling*) Thank you. (*Staring up at the spot bar*) I'm going to take
this frost out of here, Raymond. I hate it. Passionately. I can't live with a
frost up here, I'm sorry . . . (*Aware that Guy is still with him, drawing him
aside, quietly*) Guy. Just let me say this. You're going to be sensational,
boy. No doubt of it. Just do what you've been doing in rehearsal. The
audience are going to lift your game, anyway. You're home and dry . . .

*During the last, a couple of the stage management, now in costume, have
brought Dafydd the ladders which they set up for him*

Guy Dafydd, it's not the show I'm talking about . . .
Dafydd (*indicating the ladders*) Would you steady this, I just want to alter
something. Ta.

Dafydd shins up the ladders. Guy steadies them reluctantly

(*From the top of the ladders*) Now's your chance to get your own back. Tip
me off if you want to.
Guy (*wearily*) I don't want to do that, Dafydd.
Dafydd Ah well, all I can say is, it's a good job it's you down there. There's
a whole committee of them back there would do it with pleasure.

*Jarvis comes on from backstage with part of his costume on. He still has his
everyday trousers on*

Jarvis Hey! Is this right?
Dafydd (*barely glancing*) Great, Jarvis. Knockout.
Jarvis These aren't the right trousers, of course . . . (*He indicates his
trousers*)
Dafydd No, no, obviously. It's burnt out, this. (*He comes down the ladder
and examines the frost he has removed from the lamp*)
Jarvis Nor do they appear to have sent me any boots. The girl's having a
look . . .
Dafydd Oh, dear . . .
Jarvis I asked specifically for boots. I wanted some boots. The man's a
gaoler, he'd have boots. He'd never have shoes, not in a gaol . . .
Dafydd Don't worry, Jarvis, we'll find you some boots, don't worry . . .
Jarvis Well, I'm not playing him in shoes, that's all. I need to find some
boots . . .

Jarvis exits

Dafydd It would help if he found his bloody lines for a kick off. (*Yelling*)

Finished with the ladders! (*He shows Guy the frame*) Warped. Look at that, eh? (*He starts to move back towards the lighting box*)

As Dafydd does so, Ian, dressed in his street clothes, strolls in. He carries the evening paper

Dafydd (*to Ian*) What time's this, then? What time's this?
Ian (*rather aggressively*) Not on till Act Two, am I?
Dafydd Fair enough. Fair enough.
Ian (*to Guy*) Seen the paper, then?
Guy No. I've not really had time.
Ian All over the front page. I shouldn't think it'd be much of a surprise to you. There you are. "Closure Shock". (*To Dafydd*) BLM's closing ...
Dafydd What's that?
Ian (*holding up the paper*) BLM. Closing down ...

Rebecca enters and stands listening

Dafydd Closing down?
Ian That's what it says ... Five hundred jobs gone.
Dafydd Oh dear, oh dear ...
Ian They're relocating one hundred and thirty ...
Guy One hundred and twenty-eight actually.
Ian Oh, you did know then?
Guy Oh, yes.
Ian I bet you bloody did. Don't miss a trick, do you?
Rebecca How long have you known this?
Guy Since I found the note on my desk this morning. Along with most of us. (*Looking at them*) It's true.
Ian (*moving away*) I believe you, sunshine ...
Guy It's true.
Ian Sure, sure, sure ...

Ian exits backstage

Guy (*angrily, after him*) If it makes you feel any better, I don't happen to have been included in the hundred and twenty-eight ...
Rebecca I'm hardly surprised ... (*To Dafydd, indicating her costume*) Do you think this is all right, Dafydd? Since I'm bound to be standing behind some huge tree or something it probably doesn't matter, anyway.
Dafydd That's super, Beccy, super ...
Rebecca You actually like it?
Dafydd It's just right.
Rebecca (*moving off*) Oh, well. It's your production, darling. If you're expecting laughs, you won't be disappointed, will you? (*To someone offstage, as she goes*) I told you he would. He likes it ...

Rebecca exits

Dafydd (*yelling*) Come on. Let's get underway. How are you doing, Raymond? Dare I ask? (*He walks into the ladders*) I have requested these ladders be moved. Why haven't they? Bridget, somebody. Please.

Dafydd moves back to Guy who is sitting very miserably in one corner of the stage

   Bridget enters briskly

Dafydd goes to perch on a table to chat to Guy

Dafydd Guy, I'm desperately sorry to ...

Bridget whisks the table from under Dafydd. Dafydd sits wearily beside Guy

   Bridget exits after placing the table

   I'm desperately sorry to hear all this, Guy. I really am. Is that what you wanted to tell me, just now? God, I'm sorry. It's just like I said, isn't it? Here we are, playing around with pretty lights and costumes held together with safety pins. Out there it's all happening. (*More positively*) You'll be OK. I know you will. Don't despair, old friend. (*He clasps Guy affectionately round the shoulders*) Excuse me, I'm gong to have to light a few fireworks back there ...

   Dafydd exits. The stage managers return and move the ladders off. Fay comes on with Guy's wig and a small mirror

Fay (*handing these to Guy, coolly*) Here.
Guy Oh, thank you so much ...
Fay She's done what she can with it ...
Guy (*busying himself, examining the wig*) This is fine. Absolutely fine.
Fay You must be feeling pretty pleased with yourself.
Guy How do you mean?
Fay You seem to have succeeded in making fools of most people, haven't you?
Guy I don't think I have ... I didn't intend to.
Fay Calculating little bastard, aren't you? Well, you certainly fooled me. Congratulations. That doesn't often happen. You didn't really convince Ian, I'm afraid. He said you were a shit from the start ...
Guy (*hurt*) Thanks.

A silence

   The cast begin to assemble onstage. First Rebecca. Then Jarvis and then Hannah. All ignore Guy. Jarvis has found some boots from somewhere. He busies himself putting these on. Rebecca hums tunelessly. Bridget comes in to wait. She is followed by Mr Ames

Bridget He's coming in a second. He's talking to Ian.

Rebecca looks at Fay. The silence continues

   Ted and Enid enter. They alone seem blissfully unaware of the atmosphere

Enid (*as she comes on, loudly*) Oh yes, they're all ... Oh. (*Aware of the silence, in an undertone to Ted*) They're all out here ...

Pause

(*Whispering*) I think we're waiting for Dafydd.

Ted (*whispering*) Yes.

Enid (*indicating Ted's neckware*) Is your bit all right? Do you want me to tie it again?

Ted No, it's perfect now. Perfect.

Pause

These shoes are a bit tight.

Enid Oh, dear.

Ted I was supposed to have some boots but somebody's pinched them . . .

Enid Oh, dear.

Linda enters

Oh, that's better, Linda. That's much better. (*To Ted*) She's taken the ribbon off it. It's better.

Ted Much better . . .

Dafydd enters, somewhat subdued

Dafydd Sorry, everyone but . . . (*He trails away, his mind obviously else-where*) Right. Sorry. Here we go then. This is a technical run mostly for stage management and lighting and so on. But, nonetheless, do please feel free to stop if there's anything at all . . . that . . . er . . . is worrying you. At all. So. Yes. Right. Off we go. Good luck.

Everyone begins to disperse in various directions

Guy is one of the last to leave, having first put on his wig

Bridget (*yelling as she goes*) Act One beginners, stand by please . . .

Dafydd and Guy are alone onstage

Dafydd (*approaching Guy; in an undertone*) Ian's just told me, you bastard. About you and Hannah. I just want you to know, I think you are a total and utter bastard. And my one prayer is that one of these days, you'll get what's coming to you. OK? That's all I have to say to you.

Dafydd moves off towards the lighting box. Guy stands still

(*Turning as he goes*) Having said that, all the very best of luck for the show and I hope it goes really well for you. Good luck. (*As he goes*) Come on, Raymond. Let's have the opening state, please . . . Come on. Lights and music.

Dafydd exits

Guy is left onstage. The Lights close down to him alone. Prison cell lighting comes up as music starts under

Guy is joined as he speaks by Hannah as Polly and Linda as Lucy. We are gradually into the first performance of the production, near the end of Act Three, Scene XV

Guy (*as Macheath*) My dear Lucy. My dear Polly. Whatsoever hath passed between us is now at an end. If you are fond of marrying again, the best advice I can give you, is to ship yourselves off to the West Indies, where you'll have a fair chance of getting a husband a-piece; or by good luck, two or three, as you like best.

Hannah (*as Polly*) How can I suppport this sight!

Linda (*as Lucy*) There is nothing moves one so much as a great man in distress.

Linda (*singing*)	Would I might be hang'd!
Hannah	And I would so too!
Linda	To be hang'd with you.
Hannah	My dear, with you.
Guy	O Leave me to thought! I fear! I doubt! I tremble! I droop! See, my courage is out.
Hannah	No token of love?
Guy	See, my courage is out.
Linda	No token of love?
Hannah	Adieu.
Linda	Farewell.

Guy But hark! I hear the Toll of the Bell . . . etc.

During the song the action has moved to Tyburn. A scaffold has been erected. Essentially this is the platform that was centre stage at the start of the play with the addition of a gallows arm. A hooded hangman, (Dafydd), stands waiting there as the rest of the opera is played out

Jarvis enters, as the Gaoler

Jarvis Four women more, Captain, with a child a-piece! See here they come. (*He gestures*)

Rebecca, Bridget, Fay and Enid enter with prop babies, making baby-crying noises as they come

Guy (*as Macheath*) What—four wives more! This is too much. Here—tell the Sherriff's Officers I am ready.

A long drumroll. The women hurl aside their babies and with a hiss of anticipation join the rest of the company around the scaffold platform. Guy, flanked by two guards (Crispin and a stage manager) approaches. He steps up. The hangman prepares to place the noose around his neck. The sound of the crowd and the drumroll increase in volume. Guy takes a last look around; at the hangman, at the noose and, finally, at the company that has now assembled. A faint look of apprehension passes over his face as he notes their eager faces

Suddenly Ted, as the Player, appears, apart from the crowd

Ted (*as Player, with a cry*) Wait!

Total silence. All on stage, with the exception of Guy, freeze totally. Guy looks slowly around him

Ted and Mr Ames, after a moment, also unfreeze

(*To Mr Ames*) Honest friend. I hope you don't intend that Macheath shall be really executed.

Mr Ames (*as Begger, at the piano*) Most certainly, Sir. To make the piece perfect, I was for doing strict poetical justice. Macheath is to be hang'd; and for the other personages of the drama, the Audience must have suppos'd they were all either hang'd or transported.

Ted Why then, friend, this is down-right deep tragedy. The catastrophe is manifestly wrong, for an opera must end happily. All this we must do to comply with the taste of the town.

Mr Ames Your objection, sir, is very just; and is easily remov'd. For you must allow, that in this kind of drama, 'tis no matter how absurdly things are brought about. So ... (*He snaps his fingers and gestures like a magician*)

Ian rushes on in his Matt of the Mint costume, brandishing an official document

Ian A reprieve! A reprieve for Macheath!

All (*in an awed murmur*) A reprieve?

Ian gives the document to the hangman who reads it

Hangman A reprieve!

All A reprieve for Macheath!

A great deal of cheering. The gallows arm is removed. All push forward to congratulate the prisoner. The hangman, removing his hood, reveals he is Dafydd. He embraces Guy

A serving wench brings ale for them both

Guy (*as Macheath, holding up his hands for silence*) So, it seems, I am not left to my choice, but must have a wife at last. Look ye, my dears, we will have no controversie now. Let us give this day to mirth, and I am sure she who thinks herself my wife will testifie her joy by a dance.

All Come, a dance—a dance.

Guy (*singing*)   Thus I stand like a Turk, with his doxies around;
From all sides their glances his passion confound;
For, black, brown and fair, his inconstancy burns,
And the different beauties subdue him by turns:
Each calls forth her charms, to provoke his desires:
Though willing to all; with but one he retires.
But think of this maxim, and put off your sorrow,
The wretch of to-day, may be happy to-morrow.

Chorus   But think of this maxim etc.

This time, as with "The Beggar's Opera" itself, the performance ends happily and triumphantly (if a trifle cynically). The actors take their curtain calls. As the curtain falls for the last time they embrace each other, most especially their hero of the night, Guy himself

Relieved and exhausted, they return to their dressing rooms

CURTAIN

FURNITURE AND PROPERTY LIST

ACT I

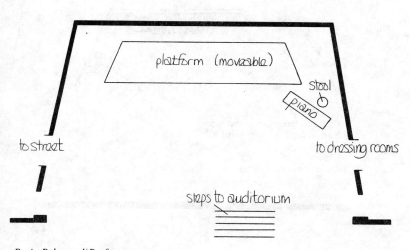

platform (moveable)

stool

piano

to street

to dressing rooms

steps to auditorium

Basic Rehearsal/Performance set

Bare stage with raised platform (easily struck)
Upright piano (moveable for Pub scene)
Piano stool
Table
Chair for prompt
Other chairs for cast

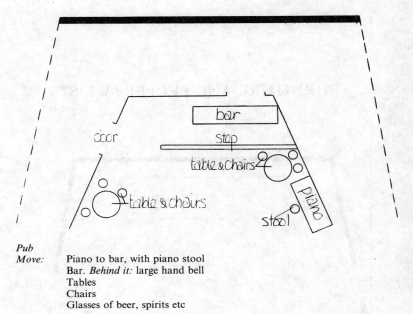

Pub
Move: Piano to bar, with piano stool
             Bar. *Behind it:* large hand bell
             Tables
             Chairs
             Glasses of beer, spirits etc

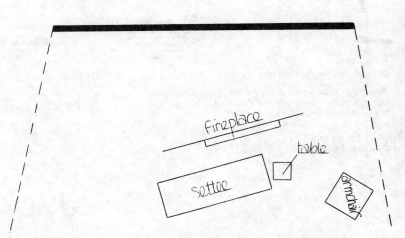

Dafydd's sitting room

Settee
Armchair. *In it:* large life-size rag doll
Fireplace
Table
General clutter and overcrowding

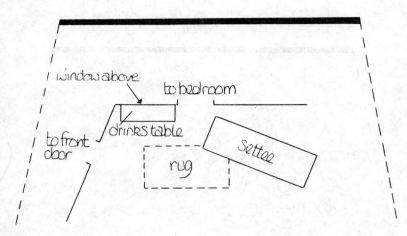

Fay's sitting room

Settee
Table
Window with curtains
Mirror

Street lamp

Off stage: Two bouquets **(Stage Management)**
               Guy's ordinary clothes, including mackintosh with an envelope containing
                   a letter and a piece of music in pocket **(Hannah)**
               Small table **(Bridget)**
               Tray. *On it:* two mugs of cocoa **(Hannah)**
               Pint of milk **(Bridget)**
               Two cups of tea **(Hannah)**
               Two exotic drinks **(Fay)**
               Bottle of Tequila **(Ian)**
               Three exotic drinks **(Fay)**
               Four papier mâché tankards **(Ted, Crispin, Jarvis and Guy)**

Personal: **Mr Ames:** rehearsal book

              Ted: rehearsal book
              Fay: cigarettes, handbag, watch
              Dafydd: script (for Guy)
              Bridget: prompt book
              Ian: evening paper
              Hannah: rehearsal book
              Enid: rehearsal book

ACT II

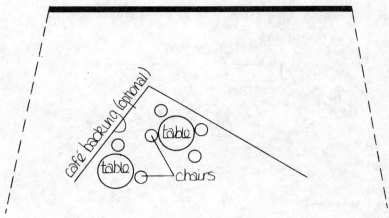

Café

Table. *On it:* used cups and saucers. Cake stand with cakes
Four chairs
Other dressing as desired

Rehearsal room

Free standing jail door
Gallows arm with noose

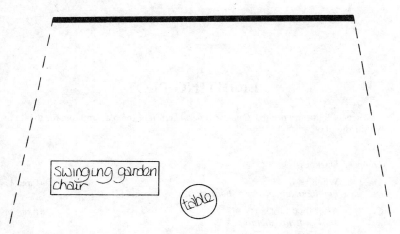

Rebecca's Garden

Garden seat
Garden table. *On it:* glass for Rebecca, cigarette box, small handbell

Off stage: Shopping bags. *In one:* paper bag containing paisley patterned pants **(Fay)**
              Beaker of tea **(Dafydd)**
              Lighting plan **(Dafydd)**
              Ladder **(Stage Management)**
              Guy's wig and mirror **(Fay)**
              Four mock babies **(Enid, Fay, Rebecca, Bridget)**
              Offical document **(Ian)**
              Tray of ale **(Serving Wench)**

Personal: **Hannah:** handbag
             Fay: handbag
             Jarvis: personal stereo and headphones
             Rebecca: watch
             Guy: envelope containing "money"
             Ian: evening paper

LIGHTING PLOT

Two sets of lights are needed. One for general action of the play and one for the "play within the play"

ACT I

To open: Darkness

Cue 1	When ready *Full lights up on stage (both sets)*	(Page 1)
Cue 2	After final tableau *Darken lights slightly*	(Page 1)
Cue 3	After Company re-arranged in tableau *Lights up for curtain call (repeat as necessary)*	(Page 1)
Cue 4	After cast and audience acknowledge Guy *Lights dim to indicate final curtain*	(Page 2)
Cue 5	When ready *Extinguish "stage" lights and replace with "working" lights*	(Page 2)
Cue 6	Piano plays *"Youth's the Season Made for Joys"* *Lighting change to indicate flash-back*	(Page 3)
Cue 7	**Dafydd:** "Right. Away we go." *Lighting change to pub scene*	(Page 10)
Cue 8	**Crispin** and **Bridget** kiss *Lighting change to Dafydd's sitting-room*	(Page 17)
Cue 9	As Dafydd stands savouring the night air *Lighting change to rehearsal room. Ted only lit*	(Page 26)
Cue 10	**Ted** (*singing*): "He steals your whole estate." *Lights up to full rehearsal state*	(Page 26)
Cue 11	**Hannah** kisses **Guy** *Darken lights slightly. When Guy leaves bring up on Enid whilst remaining on Hannah*	(Page 33)
Cue 12	**Enid** and **Hannah** (*singing together*): ". . . must have done." *Lights cross fade to Fay's sitting-room*	(Page 34)
Cue 13	**Ian:** "Bloody hellfire." *Fade light on Ian. Bring up moonlit street effect*	(Page 38)
Cue 14	During **Guy**'s song (as Matt) *Lights change to rehearsal room*	(Page 38)
Cue 15	**Guy** rises to follow the others off *Fade to black-out*	(Page 40)

ACT II

To open: Lights on Macheath (**Crispin**)

Cue 16	At end of Macheath song	(Page 41)
	Crossfade to cafe	
Cue 17	**Guy** exits unhappily	(Page 45)
	Fade light on cafe. Bring up light on Linda	
Cue 18	**Linda** (*singing*): ". . . worried, crushed and shaken."	(Page 45)
	Bring up general light on rehearsal	
Cue 19	**Rebecca:** "Do it? He'd love it."	(Page 54)
	Close to single spot on Guy	
Cue 20	**Guy** (*singing*): ". . . t'other wife would take ill."	(Page 54)
	Lights up on Rebecca's garden	
Cue 21	**Guy** shifts uncomfortably	(Page 55)
	Lights fade on garden. Up on Ted, Enid and Jarvis	
Cue 22	At end of song	(Page 55)
	Fade on Ted, Enid and Jarvis. Up again on garden	
Cue 23	**Guy** pockets envelope	(Page 57)
	Fade on garden. Lights up on rehearsal	
	NB Second set of lights needed here to light production	
Cue 24	**Dafydd:** ". . . a half-wit, he should. . ."	(Page 58)
	*Single light comes up (vivid orange)	
Cue 25	**Dafydd:** ". . . bloody numbers, these plans."	(Page 58)
	*Single light up	
Cue 26	**Dafydd:** "Your number eighteen."	(Page 58)
	*Another lamp on	
Cue 27	**Guy:** ". . . over a week to learn the thing."	(Page 59)
	Brilliant light on Guy and Hannah	
Cue 28	**Hannah:** "Well, when can we?"	(Page 59)
	*Two more lights on Guy and Hannah	
Cue 29	**Hannah:** ". . . cares about Dafydd."	(Page 60)
	*More lights on Guy and Hannah	
Cue 30	**Hannah:** ". . . nothing to do with it."	(Page 60)
	*Lights on Guy and Hannah's knees	
Cue 31	**Guy:** "That just isn't true."	(Page 60)
	*More lights come up	
Cue 32	**Dafydd:** "Show me something else."	(Page 61)
	Various lights flash on and off (see pages)	
Cue 33	**Guy:** "I love you, Hannah."	(Page 62)
	Romantic light comes up	
Cue 34	**Guy** is left, miserable	(Page 62)
	Lights revert to near normal level	

Cue 35	**Guy:** ". . . ridiculous time to say it but . . ." *Lights switch to working level*	(Page 63)
Cue 36	**Guy** is left alone *Lights close down on Guy. Prison cell light comes up*	(Page 67)
Cue 37	During song *Lights change to Tyburn scene*	(Page 67)
Cue 38	At end of performance *Curtain calls*	(Page 68)
Cue 39	Cast return to dressing-room *Fade to black-out*	(Page 68)

*Kill these lights when appropriate

EFFECTS PLOT

ACT I

Cue 1   As "Curtain" falls   (Page 1)
Muffled applause, growing louder as "Curtain" rises again (repeat as necessary)

Cue 2   **Dafydd** raises his hand for silence   (Page 2)
Cease applause

Cue 3   **Dafydd** presents Guy   (Page 2)
Renewed applause

Cue 4   After lights dim to indicate final curtain   (Page 2)
Applause dies away

Cue 5   **Guy** surveys darkened stage   (Page 3)
Piano fragment of "Youth's the Season Made for Joys"

Cue 6   After lighting change 6   (Page 3)
Laughter and voices from dressing-room

Cue 7   **Guy:** "... when does it start? Open?"   (Page 11)
Faint ring of telephone

Cue 8   **Dafydd:** "God damn it."   (Page 18)
Door slam

Cue 9   **Dafydd:** "... you should be in BLM because—"   (Page 23)
Telephone rings

Cue 10   **Ian:** "... and say we both could ... OK?"   (Page 37)
Doorbell rings

ACT II

Cue 11   **Guy:** "... I am ready."   (Page 67)
Long drum roll, continuing

MADE AND PRINTED IN GREAT BRITAIN BY
LATIMER TREND & COMPANY LTD, PLYMOUTH
MADE IN ENGLAND